MEETING THE WHALES

THE EQUINOX GUIDE TO GIANTS OF THE DEEP

ERICH HOYT

WITH ILLUSTRATIONS BY PIETER FOLKENS

CAMDEN HOUSE

To Alexandra and to Richard

© Copyright 1991 Erich Hoyt

Canadian Cataloguing in Publication Data

Hoyt, Erich, 1950-
    Meeting the whales

ISBN 0-921820-25-9 (bound) ISBN 0-921820-23-2 (pbk.)

1. Whales – Juvenile literature.   I. Title.

QL737.C4H6   1991   j599.5   C91-093134-8

Front Cover: François Gohier

Back Cover: E.R. Degginger, Bruce Coleman Inc.

Trade distribution by
Firefly Books
250 Sparks Avenue
Willowdale, Ontario
Canada M2H 2S4

Printed and bound in Canada by
D.W. Friesen & Sons Ltd.
Altona, Manitoba, for
Camden House Publishing
(a division of Telemedia Publishing Inc.)
7 Queen Victoria Road
Camden East, Ontario K0K 1J0

Designed by: Andrew McLachlan

Colour separations by
Hadwen Graphics
Ottawa, Ontario

Printed on acid-free paper

Contents

Introduction

Early one summer morning a few years ago, I watched from the deck of a ship as a mother humpback whale and her calf floated in the long swells of the North Atlantic. The two whales nuzzled each other in apparent affection. They spouted, a big blow and a little blow, sucked air into their lungs and dipped into the sea.

I thought they were gone. But as I peered down into the blue-green water, the whales suddenly came into view. The calf was pressing its lips to its mother's belly, trying to nurse.

Watching the humpbacks, I reflected on how whales, like us, are social mammals. In the fourth century B.C., the Greek philosopher Aristotle declared that whales and dolphins have a great deal more in common with humans than they do with fish and other sea creatures. He knew that they are warm-blooded and air-breathing like land mammals. As do humans and other mammals, whales give birth—after a long pregnancy—to helpless babies that take all of the mother's attention for weeks and much of her concern for many months, sometimes a year or more. In time, the infants learn how to feed themselves and how to survive in a new world. But living as social mammals, they spend much of their time in the company of their own kind.

Yet whales differ from land mammals, mainly in that they live in an environment which, at least to humans, is the most foreign and forbidding on Earth: the deep ocean. It was not always so. About 50 million years ago, the four-legged ancestors of whales lived on land. These dog-to-bear-sized mammals also gave rise to hoofed

descendants such as deer, sheep and goats. Over the years, the whales' ancestors began to spend more and more time in rivers and in the sea, perhaps to search for more food or to escape predators.

Like all animals and plants on Earth, early whales were evolving to meet their new circumstances even as they kept their identities—in this case, as warm-blooded mammals. At first, they no doubt returned to land from the water from time to time; they had to come to the surface for air. To maintain a warm body temperature in chilly waters, they grew an outer fat layer called blubber—up to 50 centimetres thick—a feature that cold-blooded fish did not need. Millions of years in the sea served to

streamline the whales: they lost their hind legs, and their "arms" became flippers; their tails developed into powerful propulsion machines. They became champion swimmers and divers capable of feats that humans, with the help of submarines and other deep-sea exploration vehicles, have only recently begun to challenge. And they grew to awesome sizes—as much as 30 metres in length and 144 tonnes in weight.

In this underwater world, hearing became the most important sense. Although many whale species are thought to have good vision, it is hard to see below the surface of the sea, especially at the depths where some species feed. But sound travels well through water, and whales use it to

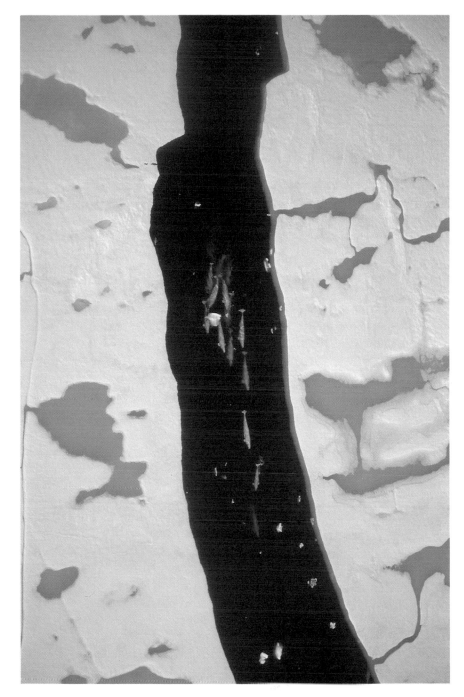

The blue whale, far left, the world's largest animal, has an appetite to match. The throat pleats of its lower jaw, or pouch, expand to accommodate 40 to 50 tonnes of water and krill, the five-to-eight-centimetre-long shrimplike animals that it lives on. In seconds, as the blue continues swimming, it will squeeze the water out the sides of its mouth and swallow the krill.

For as many as eight or nine months of the year, the blue whale, a mostly solitary feeder, will dine in cold waters. Here, ocean upwellings create explosions of plankton and the krill that feed on them. In winter, blue whales migrate thousands of kilometres to warmer waters, where they mate and give birth.

The belugas, left, are following a lead through the pack ice off Baffin Island. Their all-white colouring is an adaptation for year-round life in the Arctic and probably helps camouflage them from their predators—polar bears and killer whales. Belugas live on fish; in winter, they must dive deeper to feed, sometimes hunting under the ice packs or moving to ice-free offshore waters. One of the smallest whales, a mature beluga measures up to about 4.5 metres long and weighs about 1.5 tonnes, only about 1 percent of the weight of a mature blue.

communicate with one another. Whales have also developed an ability to use sound to scan their underwater world. Using something called echolocation, or whale sonar, some species send out sounds and listen to the echoes in order to find both their food and their way.

This book explores that other world. On the following pages, you will meet about 20 different species of whales – all of those known to live in the northern hemisphere. Most of them range throughout the world ocean. Each species has adapted in its own way to life in the sea, developing unique features or strategies for survival. Each has different food and feeding habits, separate migration routes and its own niche, or place, in the sea. While we will not dwell on the closely related dolphins and porpoises, sometimes referred to as "small whales," they may be mentioned in passing as part of the large family of toothed whales. Because of their much smaller size, however, their social behaviour and other aspects of their biology are rather different.

We will focus on the origins of whales and on their senses, their remarkable swimming and diving abilities and on many facets of their behaviour. We will see why the sperm whale has its large head, why humpbacks sing songs and why the narwhal has its tusk. We will consider the relationship between people and whales, beginning with the long era when humans killed them for food and oil and examining the modern dilemma of how to coexist on a planet crowded with humanity and threatened by activities that cause air and water pollution.

In the study of animal behaviour, whales are recent subjects. Some of the questions we have about them can now be answered as a result of indepth whale research. Today, scientists are actually living with the whales, recording their daily lives in the wild and learning new things about them every year. With this knowledge, plus our help and understanding, the whale species once hunted to near extinction and reduced by habitat loss may yet be saved. This book will take you on a voyage of discovery to meet the whales, to discover their true nature and to ponder their future.

A mother and calf humpback whale, far left, swim through a tropical sea. Humpback whales get their name from the raised platform, or hump, around their dorsal fin. Their reptilelike snout, often covered with bumps and barnacles, gives them a bizarre profile, but male humpbacks sing songs that are among the most beautiful in the animal kingdom. Calves are born in winter after 11 or 12 months of pregnancy. They stay under their mother's protective, ever watchful eye for the first year and sometimes for part of the second. At only a few months of age and still nursing, they follow their mothers on a several-thousand-kilometre migration to cold temperate or polar waters. There, the calf is eventually weaned and learns to eat solid food.

Humpback whales, top left, often feed in organized groups, lunging to the surface, mouths open. These humpbacks, feeding on herring off Alaska, show their barnacle-encrusted chins as the throat grooves expand into a pouch to accommodate masses of food and water.

A blue whale skeleton, bottom left, reveals the huge jawbone of a large whale. The head can be 20 to 40 percent of the body length. The large mouth evolved to help the whale engulf enough of its spread-out, tiny prey to feed itself.

We marvel at whales not only because of their size but also because they are mammals that once lived on land. About 50 million years ago, the four-legged ancestors of whales entered the sea, but one can still see the bones of the flipper, near the centre right of the photograph, with fingerlike "digits" from its terrestrial past. Some whales even carry remnants of leg bones.

Whale Biology

How Big Are Whales?

The first thing that impresses us about whales is their size. Everything about them is big. The heart of a blue whale is the size of a sports car. The eye of a right whale is the size of a grapefruit. The 10-to-12-metre "wing-span" of a humpback includes two flippers, each up to 5 metres long — the longest "arms" in the animal kingdom. The tail of a blue whale, measured from edge to edge, can be 6 metres across. The 7.8-kilogram brain of a sperm whale is more than five times heavier than a human's.

Even baby whales start out large. At birth, a blue whale is about 7 metres long and weighs 2,500 kilograms. While nursing, it drinks 225 litres of milk daily and gains about 3.7 kilograms every hour – 90 kilograms a day. At 8 months, when the young-

ster is ready to leave its mother, it has grown to a length of 15 metres and a weight of 22.5 tonnes.

The largest animal on Earth, the blue whale can reach a length of up to 30 metres and a weight of up to 144 tonnes when it is fully grown. Not all species are quite so big. The dwarf sperm whale, for example, is 2 to 3 metres long when fully grown, about the size of a dolphin and only a little bigger than an adult human.

No one can say with certainty why the size of most whales changed so dramatically once they began to live in the sea. Certainly, they needed a thick layer of blubber to keep warm there. Likewise, in order to survive, they had to be able to swallow huge amounts of their tiny food, which called for a big mouth and, consequently, a large body.

But none of the whales' land ancestors came close to the size of a blue whale. An animal so bulky could have evolved only in the sea. Large land animals require huge limbs both to support their great weight and to enable them to move around. In the sea, however, the water buoys them up, allowing even the biggest and bulkiest animals to cavort like acrobats.

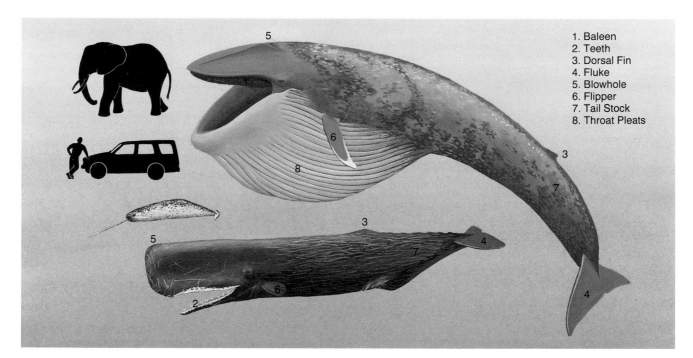

1. Baleen
2. Teeth
3. Dorsal Fin
4. Fluke
5. Blowhole
6. Flipper
7. Tail Stock
8. Throat Pleats

Kinds of Whales

Scientists often refer to whales as "cetaceans," a term that includes all whales, dolphins and porpoises. There are two types of cetaceans—toothed and baleen. Toothed whales are called *odontocetes,* a word with Greek origins that literally means "sea monsters with teeth." These include the sperm whales, belugas, narwhals and beaked whales, as well as all the dolphins and porpoises. The baleen whales—such as gray, humpback, blue and fin whales—are called *mysticetes,* which means "sea monsters with moustaches." Look at a baleen whale head-on, and you'll see what the Greeks were talking about. When the mouth is partly open, the baleen plates growing down from the roof of the mouth look like a moustache. Baleen is made of keratin, a flexible material similar to our fingernails. After the whale gulps a mouthful of food and seawater, the baleen plates trap small fish and shrimplike crustaceans called krill, allowing the water to pass out through the sides of its mouth.

The differences in feeding habits between baleen and toothed whales mean that the two groups inhabit very different areas of the ocean, some of them travelling great distances in search of food. But there are other differences. Baleen whales tend to be larger in overall size than the toothed species (there are some exceptions), while toothed whales have a larger brain-to-body-size ratio than baleen whales. The sperm whale, for example, is smaller than the blue whale, but its brain is much larger.

The two different types of whales are represented in the illustration at bottom far left: A blue whale, top, is an example of a baleen whale. A sperm whale and the much smaller narwhal, bottom, represent the toothed whales. The proportions indicate the relative size of the three species, and we can easily make size comparisons with a small car, an Asian elephant and a human, also shown.

A blue whale, seen diving in the photograph, top far left, is the largest baleen whale, and the sperm whale is the largest toothed whale. Most baleen whales are larger than toothed whales, but there are exceptions, such as the minke whale, which is closer in size to a beluga than a sperm whale.

The basic difference between baleen and toothed whales is that baleen whales have no teeth. Toothed whales feed largely on fish and squid, while baleens prefer smaller animals—using their baleen plates to strain a mouthful of krill, copepods and small schooling fish. Many, though not all, baleen whales have throat pleats that allow their mouths to expand when eating to get a bigger mouthful of such small food; those whales which do not have expanding mouths, like bowhead and right whales, tend to have extremely large mouths anyway. But toothed whales never have throat pleats.

At left, a minke whale opens its mouth to reveal its baleen plates. As the smallest baleen whale, the minke whale has the shortest baleen, only up to about 20 centimetres long. There is just enough room for water to pass out of the mouth between the plates without letting the krill and small fish escape.

Fact & Fiction

In the well-known biblical story, Jonah is swallowed by a whale and lives for days in its belly before being cast upon a distant shore. The story has inspired art and literature for centuries, but is it fact or fiction? Could Jonah have survived inside a giant whale?

Some illustrations of the Jonah story feature a whale that looks like a sperm whale. Although blue whales are larger than the sperm, they do not have teeth and consequently eat nothing bigger than krill, which are no more than about eight centimetres long. A bull sperm whale, up to 18 metres long, is probably the only whale capable of swallowing a human whole.

Shy and not considered dangerous, the sperm nevertheless sometimes caused trouble for early whalers. Trying to harpoon a 40-tonne animal from a small boat could be a problem, sometimes resulting in an overturned craft. In at least one documented case, a whaler was knocked overboard and into the mouth of a thrashing sperm whale, never to be seen by his mates again. Even if the sperm had been immediately pulled on deck and cut open, the man would have been dead from suffocation. He would also have been almost unrecognizable: within minutes, the whale's stomach acids would have begun the digestive process.

Ever since humans began to tell stories, whales have been the source of many other fables, fantasies and pure fiction. Whales were once thought to be either fish that spouted water or sea monsters. The broken-off tusk of the narwhal, found on northern beaches, was believed to be the horn of the fabled unicorn. Although Aristotle determined as early as the fourth century B.C. that whales were mammals, people continued to believe what they preferred to believe rather than what was true.

Yet the truth about whales is sometimes stranger than fiction. The narwhal's tusk is actually a three-metre-long tooth that erupts through its upper lip. The largest whale, the blue, can eat nothing bigger than an orange, and a humpback may carry half a tonne of barnacles on its body. Speculating about the logistics of swimming 16,000 kilometres in over a few months during the course of

a migration—a stunt performed annually by gray whales—reminds us that the scale of true whale tales is staggering.

Modern myths, believed by large numbers of people, include the notion that whales are starting to talk to scientists and that soon there will be a whale-human dictionary. Although some small whales and dolphins have proved to be surprisingly good mimics of various sounds and to be easy to train by means of human speech, whistles or hand signals, we are far from being able to communicate with them as we do with fellow humans. Yet whales may one day amaze us in this matter as well.

In one pictorial version of the story of Jonah and the whale, far left, Jonah is thrown to the whale. It all started when Jonah refused God's request for him to go to Nineveh to preach against the city's wickedness. Sometime later, when Jonah was aboard a boat, a big storm arose and whales approached. In this depiction, they look more like sea monsters. Jonah's fellow sailors were terrified: they prayed for mercy, and they threw out barrels to try to appease the whales and calm the sea. When that did not work, they tossed out Jonah. The whale swallowed him and, after three days, spat him out on the shore. Jonah, of course, headed straight for Nineveh. The city was spared, and no more whales bothered Jonah.

The skull of a rare two-tusked narwhal, left, is an example of the truth about whales being stranger than fiction. The tusk itself is a tooth that erupts through the upper lip and grows to about three metres long. Only rare individuals have two tusks—perhaps 1 in 500 males. Tusk size appears to be the mark of dominance in the males. In one of nature's unexplained quirks, a few females have tusks, and there is at least one case of a female with two tusks.

Where Did Whales Come From?

Scientists can reconstruct the ancient origins and long histories of animals through fossils found in rocks. By comparing fossils from different time periods, they can piece together how creatures evolved. Some animals, however, have only bits of their history preserved as fossils. There are many gaps in the fossil record of whales. In fact, most of the early whale species that led to modern whales are now extinct. Such extinctions, occurring over millions and millions of years, are part of the process of evolution.

About 50 million years ago, sometime after the extinction of the dinosaurs, the first whale-type animals entered the shallow seas around northeast Africa and what is now Saudi Arabia. Most of these archeocetes (ARK-ee-oh-seats), as they are called, were small compared with modern whales, but some may have been up to 20 metres long. They had long snouts, paddlelike flippers, small legs or hind limbs and a long tail that could move up and down. Generally, they lived in the water and caught slow-moving fish and shellfish. The recent discovery of an archeocete called *Basilosaurus isis* shows that 40 million years ago, some ancestral whales living full-time in the water still had hind limbs.

The archeocetes evolved from land-dwelling animals called mesonychids (mess-oh-NICK-ids). Mesonychids were bulky animals that ate mainly meat, but some were specialized, plant-eating ungulates (animals with cloven hoofs). Thus whales and modern animals such as deer, sheep and goats appear to have a common ancestor.

Between about 25 and 38 million years ago, the archeocetes were replaced by at least four different families of whales—two were primitive toothed species, and two were primitive baleens. Whether the toothed and baleen whales branched off from archeocetes or whether they developed independently is not known. After several million years in the water, these species evolved special nostrils, called blowholes, that moved back to a position high on the head. At the same time, flaps developed to cover the blowholes and to keep out the water when the whales were submerged. As they lost all of their fur and most of their hair, their bodies became more streamlined.

The teeth of the primitive toothed whales, once divided into incisors, canines and grinding teeth like those of their land ancestors, became uniform. The toothed whales also developed skulls with specialized structures for sending and receiving sound: this was crucial for hunting in deep

water. The primitive baleen whales, meanwhile, lost their teeth. Instead, they grew rows of baleen plates from the upper gums, similar to those of modern baleen whales. These specialized structures were ideal for catching small fish and the krill that were then becoming abundant.

By about 25 million years ago, the primitive toothed and baleen whales had colonized the sea, adapting to new environments and further evolving. The sperms branched off from the other toothed whales and were the first to assume their present form, early in the Miocene epoch, about 23 million years ago. The beaked whales, too, appear to have branched off early and developed as a separate family.

About 15 million years ago, a primitive dolphin family known as kentriodonts evolved into most of the toothed species that we know today. A few million years later, the baleen whales evolved into their modern forms. The mouth became bigger, and the forehead extended to allow the mouth to open wider. The baleen grew even longer – up to 4.2 metres in the bowhead whale – and in some cases, throat pleats developed to allow the mouth to expand even wider. As the mouth grew larger, the body had to get bigger to support it. The wide range of adaptations is extraordinary, from the 9-metre-long minke whale to the 30-metre-long blue whale, from the humpback with a great expanding throat to the right whale with a head that is all mouth.

Some species, such as gray whales, may have evolved fairly recently. The earliest-known gray whale fossils go back only to the late Pleistocene, less than two million years ago. At that time, grays looked exactly as they do today.

Four stages in the evolution of whales are shown in this illustration, from left to right. About 50 million years ago, the first whale ancestors to venture into the sea were animals called mesonychids. They had four legs and a tail more suited to a land mammal, but they had a taste for seafood. A few million years later, in the Eocene epoch, a primitive archeocete family called protocetus evolved—ancestral whales with streamlined bodies and tails for propulsion underwater.

About 38 million years ago, early in the Oligocene epoch, the dorudontines appeared. These were medium-sized toothed whales. During the same period, many other kinds of whales were evolving. But it was not until late in the Oligocene, more than 25 million years ago, that the immediate ancestors of modern whales evolved with teeth and baleen similar to those of whales today.

Early in the Miocene, which began 25 million years ago, modern families of baleen and toothed whales appeared as some of the species we know today. (Sperm and beaked whales were among the first to arrive. Gray whales may be the most recent.)

Four main families of baleen whales and ten families of toothed whales, including the dolphins and porpoises, have survived. Today, we still see evidence of the ancestors of modern whales. A young humpback caught by whalers some years ago off Vancouver Island had 1.2-metre-long hind legs. As new fossils are found and classified, the picture of evolution changes. In recent years, scientists have also begun to study the genetic differences among whales, which may eventually help to clarify their evolutionary paths.

From a small boat, I once watched a lumbering humpback accelerate in the heat of battle on the mating grounds off Hawaii. The 40-tonne animal was transformed from a "gentle giant" to a bulky torpedo in a few short seconds. Top sprinting speed for a humpback might be as fast as 30 kilometres per hour.

Whales are impressive swimmers and divers. Among large species, blue, fin and sei whales are the fastest, cruising on migration at speeds of 4 to 30 kilometres per hour. One tagged sei was tracked over 3,200 kilometres at an average speed of more than 17 kilometres per hour. But even slower-moving whales are faster than human swimmers.

Scientists are only beginning to discover clues about how whales are able to move so quickly and maintain speed for such great distances, sometimes thousands of kilometres. The shape of their bodies helps. Even the fattest northern rights, when seen from the air, are revealed as surprisingly streamlined – although not nearly as streamlined as the blue whales. Compared with ships, whales have flexible bodies. Their thick blubber, unattached to muscle, can bend and bulge in response to water pressure, reducing the turbulence created as they move through the water and lessening the overall drag.

Yet when the blubber is overly thick, it can limit how fast the animal is able to swim. The average blubber thickness in a blue whale is much less than in a northern right whale. If a right tried to swim as fast as a blue, it would quickly overheat and die. The movement of the whale's muscles produces heat that is trapped by the insulating layer of blubber. The thicker the blubber, the more heat is trapped. Baleen whales lose some of their blubber layer during a long winter of little feeding. On migration back to the feeding grounds, they can safely move faster – which, being hungry, is exactly what they want to do.

Some whales are deep divers. Scientists have been able to determine just how deep they usually dive by looking at the food they eat. (They do this by examining the stomachs of whales that die at sea or wash

ashore.) Humpbacks and minkes feed on small schooling fish and krill found in the topmost layer of the sea, rarely diving down more than a few hundred metres. Sperms and the various beaked species, however, eat mostly squid that live many hundreds of metres beneath the surface. Such whales can stay underwater for periods of up to an hour or more, whereas shallow-feeding species may submerge for only 5 to 10 minutes at a time. Sperm whales have been found entangled in telephone cable at depths of 1,070 metres, and they have been tracked by sonar to more than 2.4 kilometres deep, which is the known record depth for any whale. The northern bottlenose is the champion breath-holder, known to stay down for as long as two hours.

How do whales stay underwater so long and dive to depths impossible for humans? Although they have relatively small lungs and take along little air on their dives, whales appear to be able to reduce their heart rate and their need for oxygen in the brain. During a deep dive, to avoid absorbing dangerous nitrogen that would cause the bends, their lungs collapse, forcing air into the windpipe and nasal passages. Yet whales need oxygen for their muscles while they hunt in the depths. The secret lies in the presence of large amounts of a substance called myoglobin, which combines with oxygen and allows it to be stored in the muscles. Storing great quantities of oxygen right in their muscles is the safest way for whales to live the life of a deep diver.

The tail fluke is the whale's source of propulsion. The broad tail of a blue whale, top far left, up to six metres wide, is very strong; it is powered by two muscle masses, one in the upper and one in the lower region of the tail stock.

At bottom far left is a portrait of a gray whale as it breaks the surface. The spout, or blow, of a whale is air being expelled from the lungs. The spout carries water vapour from the lungs and around the blowhole and forces it into the cool air. Recent studies show that spouting may be a sort of coughing reflex to remove secretions which collect in the windpipe. When the secretions are cleared, the whale takes in fresh air.

The breathing rates and diving depths of whales vary by species, left, although both usually exceed the abilities of a human. Follow the paths of the whales in the illustration—from left to right, a gray whale, a sperm whale and a Baird's beaked whale—to see how deep they dive and how long they can stay underwater. A sperm whale, preparing to hunt giant squid in the depths, might take 50 breaths in a row, flooding its muscles with oxygen, then dive to 1,000 metres or more and remain submerged for longer than an hour. Baird's beaked whales do not dive as deep as sperm whales, but they may stay down longer—more than an hour. Gray whales are shallow divers by comparison.

How Whales Perceive Their World

In the deep, dark sea, where little light can penetrate, the whistles, screams, groans and clicks of whales echo through the ocean and across the vast ocean floor. These sounds are the key to understanding how a whale perceives and interacts with its world.

Like humans, whales use their senses to obtain information and to communicate. But because they live in a watery environment, whales use certain senses more than others. While hearing is crucial, other senses are used to a varying extent by different whale species. The thick layer of blubber does not remove the sensation of touch, and whales often use touch during social contact such as play, aggression or mating. Some of the smaller toothed whales and dolphins that have been kept in captivity seem to enjoy being touched, even with a feather. Many are known to use their flippers, flukes or mouths, including the teeth, to touch other whales. They sometimes rub against companions in play and mating rituals. Humpbacks on the mating grounds near Hawaii have been observed blowing bubbles under each other, perhaps to excite one another or to show aggression when males are chasing females.

Land animals from ants to wolves make extensive use of chemical communication. The messages, such as "follow me" or "this is my territory," are "written" in body secretions or urine, depending on the species and the message, and are smelled or tasted by members of the same species. Smell is probably rarely or never used by whales. Olfactory bulbs or nerves, which enable most land animals to smell, are absent in toothed whales and greatly reduced in baleen whales. Taste is much more useful than smell for animals that spend a lot of their time submerged. Whales' taste buds are located at the base of the tongue. Research with dolphins and other small toothed whales in aquariums has shown that while they are able to detect tiny differences in citric acid, they have difficulty tasting saltiness and sweetness. But no one knows whether whales might somehow leave messages in the water that could be tasted by other whales.

The vision of most whales is highly developed, even though it is useless at the dark depths where some regularly hunt. All species must come to

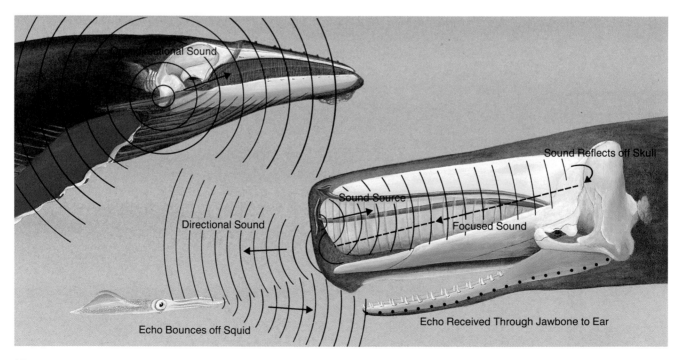

Directional Sound

Sound Source

Sound Reflects off Skull

Focused Sound

Echo Bounces off Squid

Echo Received Through Jawbone to Ear

The illustration, far left, shows the uses of sound by baleen whales and toothed whales. A typical baleen whale, such as a humpback, makes sounds that are omnidirectional—they carry through the water in every direction. Such sounds, which are also sometimes made by toothed whales, might be useful for any widely spaced animal that simply needs to keep in touch with others of its kind.

Among toothed whales, sperm whales and others also send out special directional sounds, such as clicks for hunting. By listening to the reflected echoes from squid or other prey, the whale can judge location, size, even speed of travel.

Whales produce sounds in various ways: in the nasal passages of the head by varying the opening of the nasal plug; by forcing air through a partly open blowhole; from the larynx, as in other mammals (shown as the source of sound in the baleen whale at far left); channelled through the bulbous melon, a lens-shaped body of fat and muscle in the forehead (as shown in the sperm whale) that may help to focus the sounds into a beam for echolocation.

How do whales hear? Sound waves, moving through the water, enter the whale's head and may be carried as vibrations mainly through the lower jaw to the inner ear, or bulla, like the one held in a researcher's hand, left. (This bulla came from a dead yearling gray whale that washed up along the California coast.) Surrounded by a bubbly foam, the bulla is free-floating—it is not attached to the skull. Hearing ability varies in different whale species: some hear in much the same range as humans; others can hear ultrasonic sounds, far above our range.

the surface for air, and they probably use their eyes both in the water's top light layers and above the surface to help orient themselves and to locate their mates and food. Studies show that some small toothed whales and dolphins can see as well above water as underwater. Some species can also see in colour. But the eyes of dolphin species that live in rivers are reduced to tiny slits. In muddy river water, vision is a useless sense, and over millions of years, these river dolphins have become virtually blind.

But hearing is the main sense used by most whales, and there are almost as many different kinds of sounds as there are species of whales. In general, the big whales make low sounds, and the small whales and dolphins make high sounds. Baleen whales have a hearing range close to our own; toothed whales and dolphins can hear sounds that are much higher. Blues make low-pitched moans that last 15 to 38 seconds, while minkes make a variety of grunts, thumps and clicks, each lasting less than half a second. Belugas are described as singing like canaries.

and the patterns can be studied.

A toothed whale uses echolocation by bouncing these clicks off objects in its path. The sound of the echo and how fast it returns allow the animal to construct in its brain a sound picture of the object. The object's size, shape, density and distance all affect the resonance of the echo. A large codfish, for instance, creates a different sound than does a herring. Studies of small toothed whales show that they are able to distinguish tiny differences in the size of objects such as two similar balls — differences that can barely be seen by the human eye. Echolocation has been demonstrated in only a few species of toothed whales. Some baleen whales make clicking sounds, but there is no proof that they use them as sonar.

Compared with the clicks used for echolocation, the communication signals of whales are louder, longer, lower-pitched sounds that carry great distances. Some scientists say that under the best conditions, the sounds may travel hundreds or even thousands of kilometres through the sea. In any case, even with background noise from ship traffic, underwater microphones (called hydrophones) regularly pick up sounds from submarines 80 kilometres away. No one knows whether whales use the ocean for long-distance communication or, for that matter, what the whales have to talk about. As fellow social mammals, we can only imagine that sound communication probably fulfills the basic needs of finding mates and companions, indicating distress or danger and staying in touch with the family or group.

And the different sounds can serve different purposes for the whales. They may be for navigation and for finding food, called echolocation, or for communication. They may also be songs — as are those of the humpback whale.

Echolocation consists of clicks that sound like the loud ticking of a clock or a Geiger counter alternately slowing down and speeding up. Some clicks, however, especially those produced by the smaller toothed whales and dolphins, are ultrasonic — they cannot be heard by human ears. (Your dog, capable of hearing higher pitches than humans, can hear some of them.) Scientists study the sounds by recording them on a special tape recorder and later slowing down the tape on the playback. The sounds are then audible to humans,

A gray whale, far left, presents its head to be stroked by a group of whale watchers. Whale skin is sensitive to touch, and touching is part of a whale's life starting at birth, when the newborn is lifted to the surface to take its first breath. For the first year or more, the calf will nuzzle its mother's belly to nurse. As they grow up, whales touch each other while playing, fighting and mating.

Most of the gray whales that seek out whale watchers seem to be young animals on their own. Some scientists think that they may be eager for social contact because they have recently separated from their mothers but are too young to mate. This gray whale may also be curious and simply want to look at people close up.

Although whales seem to use sound more than vision, most whales "spy hop" from time to time, sticking their heads up to look around above the water's surface. The gray whale, left, is spy hopping in one of the mating and calving lagoons of Baja California, Mexico. Whales may spy hop to look for other members of their group, to locate predators or prey or just to enjoy the view. Note that the eye of the whale is visible just above where the mouthline begins to curve down.

The Animals That Live on Whales

Most large animals, including humans, provide a home for bacteria and other small parasites. On whales, partly because they are so large, the colonies of residents can be extensive – especially various species of barnacles and cyamids, or whale lice, some of which spend their entire lives travelling aboard whales. These small animals jump onto the hosts and gain a foothold, although only a few species dig into the skin deeply enough to stay attached to the faster-moving whales and dolphins. The slower the whales move, the more barnacles and whale lice they collect. A humpback may carry thousands of barnacles weighing as much as half a tonne. The barnacles use the whale as a feeding station, while cyamids feed on the whale's skin. Neither hurts the whale. Sharp barnacles, often protruding 10 centimetres or more from the edge of the flippers and tail, may even become useful weapons when humpback males fight over females on the mating grounds in the Tropics.

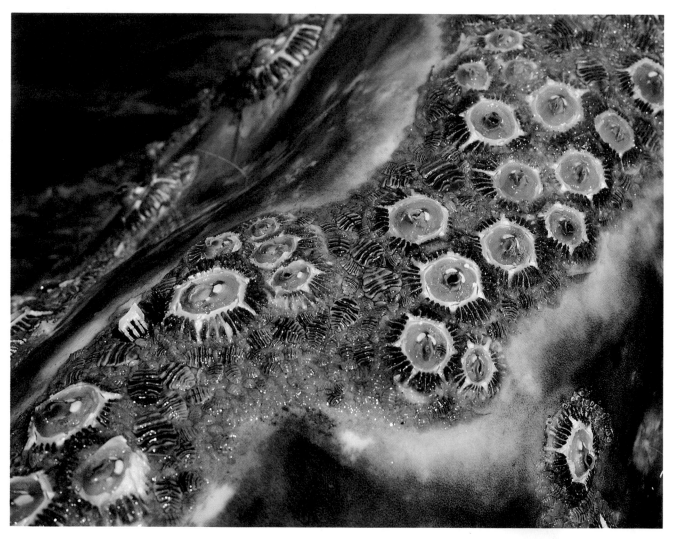

Different species of barnacles prefer different whales. The acorn barnacle colony, far left, is thriving on the head of a gray whale. Barnacles are crustaceans that live mainly on gray, humpback and other slow-moving whales. They climb aboard as larvae, perhaps attracted by a chemical scent left by their parents. Once attached, they suck part of the whale's skin into the outer cavity of their shell, forming an adhesive seal. They feed by opening their shell and waving a whiplike plume through the water, drawing plankton toward the mouth. When the whale leaps, some of the barnacles may fall off, but there are always young barnacles ready to move in.

Barnacles sometimes compete with whale lice, top left, for space on a whale's body. Whale lice, or cyamids, are also crustaceans. Less than 2.5 centimetres long, cyamids look like tiny crabs and are found on most species of baleen whales and a few toothed whales. A typical cyamid has 10 strong legs, each with a sharply curved hook at the end, which it uses to hold on to its whale host. They appear to feed on whale skin but do not harm the whale.

The stalked barnacles, bottom left, have taken up residence on the tooth of a Baird's beaked whale. Barnacles and cyamids favour the lips, chin, throat, flippers, flukes and belly of whales—mainly areas with reduced water flow. Some barnacles attach themselves to the teeth of whales, particularly beaked whales whose teeth protrude from the lower jaw and are visible even when the mouth remains closed. The stalked gooseneck barnacles grow on top of other barnacles and may protrude as much as 10 centimetres from the whale's body.

Whale Migrations

Like many animals, whales travel in search of food, mates, familiar surroundings or safe, protected areas in which to raise their young. Their journey through the ocean can be more arduous and time-consuming than the migrations of many land animals, such as birds. The journey from the Tropics, where many whale species breed and calve, to polar waters, where they do most of their eating, can be as long as 8,000 kilometres – all accomplished on an empty or nearly empty stomach.

The longest migrations are undertaken by baleen whales. Grays swim along almost the entire west coast of North America as they migrate from Mexico to Alaska. In the North Atlantic, certain northern right whales migrate from Florida or Georgia to the Bay of Fundy, while humpbacks travel from the Caribbean to the Gulf of Maine, the Gulf of St. Lawrence or Davis Strait, off Greenland.

Some toothed whales, such as sperms, likewise have widely spaced summer and winter ranges, but most do not migrate as baleen whales do from warm-water to cold-water areas and back. Certain small toothed whales and dolphins move inshore in summer and offshore in winter – a distance of only a few hundred kilometres. Some belugas travel several hundred kilometres up the rivers of the Arctic during summer, dispersing into open water in winter. Narwhals, too, venture across the Arctic to avoid getting stuck in fast-forming winter ice. But unlike most baleen whales, belugas and narwhals never visit warm temperate or tropical seas.

The conventional wisdom explaining annual long-distance migrations is that whales need warm waters to raise their young but are unable to find enough food there. Yet along with some of the toothed whales and dolphins, bowhead whales live year-round in cold waters. British scientist Peter G.H. Evans believes, in fact, that water temperature is not a crucial factor in raising calves. He suggests that calving and mating areas were adopted long ago in the whales' evolutionary histories at a time when food was plentiful in tropical seas. As the continents moved and ocean temperatures changed, the polar areas exploded with plankton and other food items, while food production in tropical seas declined. In search of nourishment, whales began to move farther and farther into polar waters. Exactly where they went and how long they stayed depended on the amount of food available and how well they adapted to arctic conditions. But in time, they established an

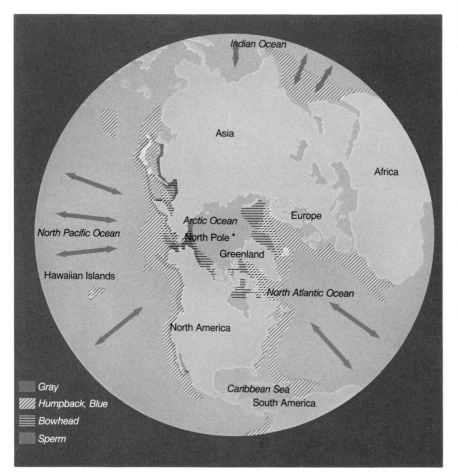

Indian Ocean

Asia

Africa

Europe

Arctic Ocean
North Pole •

Greenland

North Atlantic Ocean

North Pacific Ocean

Hawaiian Islands

North America

Caribbean Sea
South America

▨ Gray
▨ Humpback, Blue
☰ Bowhead
▨ Sperm

annual pattern of visiting cold-water areas for food in summer and returning every winter to the old calving and mating areas.

Traditional areas are common in birds and other migrating animals. Just as certain birds return to the same rock, tree or pond after a 1,500-kilometre journey every year, migrating whales often return to the same few square kilometres of ocean, be it a bay, inlet or open water along or just off the continental shelf.

British scientist Margaret Klinowska has begun to study how whales find their way through the open sea. Her theory is that they may be able to "read" geomagnetic information – the overall magnetic fields of the Earth. But to navigate in such a way, whales would also have to sense local fields and the underlying geology and to compute daily changes based on lunar, seasonal and sunspot cycles.

According to Klinowska, whales appear to move parallel to the contours of magnetic fields, perhaps setting their "biological travel clocks" every morning to account for local conditions and other changes. If whales do, indeed, have maps in their heads and timers to monitor their position and progress, nothing is known about how they might use them. To detect tiny changes in the local geomagnetic field, there would have to be a sensitive receptor system, perhaps one which uses either the small magnetic particles that have been found in the brains of whales or some unknown "receptor." For some species, such as grays, the migrations may be managed partly by trial and error. Gray whales may simply "nudge" their way along the shore from Mexico to Alaska and back, staying in coastal waters and following the contour of the land.

Solving the mysteries of how whales migrate may also help us understand why some whales strand on beaches. Klinowska has found that many strandings tend to occur where local magnetic-field lines cross an irregular coastline rather than running parallel to shores.

The great migrations of whales span the limits of every ocean from the Tropics to the poles. On the map of the northern hemisphere, far left, various probable migration routes are plotted. The migration routes of humpback and gray whales are best known. Certain right whale routes are established in the western North Atlantic. Also well studied are the paths of bowhead whales across the Arctic from Canada's Beaufort Sea in summer to the open waters of the Bering Sea in winter. Sperm whales move north and south in open-ocean areas, but the big bulls travel much farther north during the summer to feed. Most other toothed whales do not migrate but travel shorter distances in search of food or ice-free water.

The migration routes and winter mating grounds of blue, fin, sei, minke and many other whale species are largely unknown.

The gray whale parade, left, steams along the west coast of North America twice a year between the mating and calving lagoons of Mexico and the feeding grounds off Alaska, 8,000 kilometres to the north. It is one of the best known and most closely followed migrations in the animal kingdom. The whales travel in an intermittent stream that might take weeks to pass a given point. Average speed on the southward migration is two miles per hour, although they swim a little faster going north. Pregnant females and mothers with calves are the first to arrive on the feeding grounds and the last to leave. Some whales do not make the whole migration but stop off along the way—on the coast of British Columbia or northern California—to spend the summer.

Baleen Whales

Gray Whale

The young gray whale, a 2-year-old female weighing about nine tonnes, approached the small inflatable boat and raised its head out of the water. The two scientists in the boat were amazed. Once hunted almost to extinction, this whale had been called "devil fish" by whalers. Now it apparently wanted to make contact.

It was the winter of 1977, and American scientists Steven L. Swartz and Mary Lou Jones were just beginning a six-year study of gray whales in San Ignacio Lagoon, Mexico. "Amazing Grace," as they named the young female, quickly became their fast friend and a constant companion. Grace took to moving underneath the inflatable boat and lifting it clear out of the water, letting it slide off her back. Then she presented herself to be rubbed. Resting quietly beside the boat, the whale accepted a full body massage on her back, sides and head.

At first, Grace's behaviour was unique. The other grays that the researchers met were busy courting or mating, taking care of their young or participating in play groups – 20 or more pairs of socializing mothers and calves rolling around and rubbing against each other. At that point, all of the whales except Grace ignored the human observers. But in the years that followed, the researchers met more "friendlies," and the behaviour became more common. Most friendlies were juveniles, free of their mothers and perhaps looking for companionship.

One day in the early 1980s, a youngster suddenly appeared beside a boat off the west coast of Vancouver Island; perhaps it had learned to be friendly with whale-watching boats in the Mexican lagoons. It was the first time a whale had been so sociable outside of the tropical mating and calving grounds.

In fact, it is surprising that grays are friendly at all. Early whalers called them devil fish because they were known to attack skiffs. Usually, the attacker was a mother gray whose calf had been harpooned by a whaler in order to lure the large female close. This trick allowed the hunters to kill many grays. By the early 1900s, there were probably only a few thousand left, and in 1946, the species was completely protected by an agreement among the world's whaling nations.

GRAY WHALE
(*Eschrichtius robustus*)

Size: 12.0 to 13.5 metres long, up to 14.1 metres and 35 tonnes. Females slightly larger than males.

Calves at birth: About 4.9 metres and 1 to 1.5 tonnes.

Baleen: 130 to 180 yellowish plates on each side of the upper jaw. Plates grow from 5 to 25 centimetres long.

Food: Small invertebrates such as amphipods, mysids and tube worms.

Habitat: Mainly nearshore waters for migrating, lagoons for winter mating and calving. Feeds in inshore to open waters.

Range: North Pacific Ocean to the Arctic Ocean in summer.

Status: Reduced to a few thousand in the early 1900s, the eastern North Pacific population has since grown to 19,000 to 22,000.

Swimming toward the photographer, a gray whale, left, cracks the surface and sucks in a deep breath. Note that the two blowholes, characteristic of all baleen whales, are wide open. The gray whale's skin, covered with barnacles and tiny whale lice, is sometimes scarred from scraping along the seafloor for food.

Since the gray whale was protected in 1946, it has almost recovered its estimated prewhaling number of 24,000, thereby becoming one of the few success stories in whale conservation. At one time, however, there was an Atlantic gray whale that migrated all along the Atlantic seaboard from Florida to eastern Canada; today, it is extinct, and the gray whale is found only in the North Pacific.

Minke Whale

Larger than a dolphin at seven to nine metres long, the minke (pronounced MINK-ee) is the smallest baleen whale. These whales were named after an 18th-century Norwegian whaler who did not hesitate to take whales under the legal size limit. Soon, any small whale became known as one of "Minke's whales." As populations diminished, more and more of the whales that Mr. Minke and later hunters caught were this species, although they were never whaled in numbers as great as were the larger species.

Today, despite the efforts of whalers, wherever people watch whales and scientists study them, from the Arctic to the Antarctic, from the Atlantic to the Pacific, the minke hovers nearby, among the most numerous whale species. Indeed, as the larger kinds disappeared, minkes seemed to take their place, increasing in population and spreading into new areas.

Since 1980, the minke has been studied by two main research groups. Their initial goal was to determine how to identify individuals. Unlike humpbacks, minkes never lift their flukes, so it was impossible to use their tail patterns as an identification tool. The first scientists to "crack the minke code" were Eleanor D. Dorsey and her colleagues. While working off southern Vancouver Island, they found that minkes have unique scarring and light colour, or pigment, patterns on their backs and sometimes even unique marks on their dorsal fins; some of these are visible only in certain light.

At about the same time as Dorsey's study, Richard Sears, who had set out to study blue whales in the Gulf of St. Lawrence, found an accessible population of minkes just off the beach. When he couldn't find blues, as was often the case, he took minke whale photographs. He and Dorsey exchanged photographs and information on shooting techniques. Later, Sears was able to apply some of these techniques to photographing and identifying blue whales.

Through most of the 1980s, Dorsey and Sears continued to record the comings and goings of minke whales with cameras. Although they have been rewarded by seeing certain individuals return to the same areas, or home ranges, to feed year after year, the day-in, day-out work of science —

MINKE WHALE
(*Balaenoptera acutorostrata*)

Size: 7.0 to 9.0 metres long, up to 10.7 metres and about 10 tonnes. Females slightly larger than males.

Calves at birth: About 2.4 to 2.8 metres.

Baleen: 230 to 360 yellowish plates on each side of the upper jaw. Plates grow to over 20 centimetres long.

Food: Krill and small fish such as capelin, cod and herring.

Habitat: Prefers cooler waters, to the edge of the ice.

Range: World ocean.

Status: World population estimated at 505,000, with 125,000 in the northern hemisphere, mostly in the North Atlantic. Although minke whales have been killed by whalers in recent years, they appear to have increased in areas formerly used by other whales.

watching and photographing minke whales—is often slow. Minkes feed chiefly alone and sometimes in pairs. After the initial excitement of spotting a fin slicing the water, the patient scientist sees the minke roll through the water and take three or four quick breaths. Then it will disappear for three to five minutes. This pattern of very businesslike behaviour can hold for hours.

On rare occasions, though, there is a break in the tedium of observation that makes all the hours seem worthwhile. On one particular outing, Richard Sears had spent most of the day introducing whale watchers to his old minke friends near the north shore of the Gulf of St. Lawrence, an area so rich with minkes that he had nicknamed it "The Minke Way." Sears had awarded individual animals names, mostly for dorsal-fin peculiarities or back shadings, but all the names were partly whimsical. One of the first minkes Sears had ever identified had been named Bendor, for its bent dorsal fin. On this day, Sears snapped photographs as Bendor approached our boat and began to play with us. On its side, it swam back and forth beneath the boat, occasionally poking its angular, pointy head out of the water to look at us. Finally, night fell, and we were forced to leave the minke and return to camp. In a dramatic departure from the minke's often shy and standoffish behaviour, Bendor paralleled our path to shore for 15 minutes.

The minke whale, left, dives beneath the surface after taking a breath. Fairly shallow divers, minkes often stay down for only three to five minutes. When the krill or fish they seek are in deeper water, however, they dive for 20 minutes or longer.

In scientific studies off Vancouver Island and in the Gulf of St. Lawrence, researchers look for any peculiar marks on the animal's back and dorsal fin in order to identify individuals. Minkes also have pigment, or colour, patterns on their flanks and back such as those visible in this photograph. These patterns vary slightly from one minke to another, but the white band on the flippers is a characteristic of all minke whales.

Sei Whale

One of the most elusive and least studied species in the world, sei (pronounced say) whales keep mostly to the open sea. Only a handful of experienced researchers have ever had the opportunity to watch them in action, and they have yet to be adopted by a research team and made the subject of a photographic identification study – despite their distinctive backs spotted with natural splotches and slight wounds from lampreys and cookie-cutter sharks.

Yet seis, though rarely seen, are not rare. Worldwide, they are more numerous than most other large whale species. And modern whalers, combing the sea for any sign of life, were able to catch up with them and kill them when few of the larger blue and fin whales were left.

Whalers named them sei whales, after the Norwegian word for a fish we call pollack. The sei whales often appeared off northern Norway with pollack that were perhaps feeding on similar prey, such as copepods. Yet the seis are versatile feeders in terms of both prey and method. They can feed by skimming, as the northern right whale does, racing through the water open-mouthed, or, like a blue, they can gulp krill. They can also, like a humpback, chase small schooling fish. Whalers considered seis the fastest of the large whales and noted their zigzag swimming pattern.

Seis often travel in groups of two to five, although larger groups congregate in cold-water feeding areas. Every second or third year, a female gives birth to a calf.

SEI WHALE
(Balaenoptera borealis)
Size: 13.5 to 18.5 metres long, up to 21.0 metres and about 27 tonnes. Females slightly larger than males.
Calves at birth: About 4.5 metres.
Baleen: 300 to 410 dark plates on each side of the upper jaw. Plates grow up to 75 centimetres long.
Food: Copepods, krill and small fish.
Habitat: Mainly open ocean, especially temperate seas.
Range: World ocean.
Status: Whaling has cut numbers from an estimated 256,000 to 54,000 today, about 17,000 of which are in the northern hemisphere.

Bryde's Whale

Under the hot Mexican sun, American researchers Bernie Tershy, Craig Strong and Dawn Breese study whales. In the Canal de las Ballenas region of the Gulf of California, off Mexico, they watch feeding frenzies starring Bryde's (pronounced BREE-dahs) whales. The food is mainly sardines, and frenzy refers to the ravenous appetite of birds like Heermann's gulls, pelicans, blue-footed and brown boobies, as well as other creatures such as yellowfin tuna, sharks, common dolphins and Bryde's whales, all lunging for food, mouths open. All the Bryde's whales take part except for a few of the young, which are still nursing and are not yet ready to eat sardines. Instead, one curious five-metre-long calf circles the researchers' boat while its mother is eating.

Most baleen whales migrate thousands of kilometres between warm-water mating and calving grounds and cold-water feeding grounds, but Bryde's are an exception. While they may undertake short migrations, Bryde's whales stay entirely within tropical and warm temperate waters. Like some of the toothed whales, they may eat and even breed year-round in the same general area.

From time to time, Bryde's whales have made an appearance in whaling records, although many more were likely mislabelled as seis. Bryde's look very much like sei whales, only they are a little smaller. Their main distinguishing, though subtle, feature is the three ridges on the top of the head; other baleen whales have only one central ridge.

BRYDE'S WHALE
(Balaenoptera edeni)
Size: Up to 14.0 metres long. Females slightly larger than males.
Calves at birth: About 4 metres.
Baleen: 250 to 370 grey plates on each side of the upper jaw. Plates grow up to about 42 centimetres long.
Food: Schooling fish such as herring, sardines and mackerel, plus krill.
Habitat: Prefers tropical and warm temperate waters.
Range: Pacific, Atlantic and Indian oceans.
Status: Some whaling, but thought to have maintained their original population of about 90,000, of which an estimated 60,000 are found in the northern hemisphere.

Fin Whale

Fin whales, also called finbacks, often feed alone, although some prefer to travel and feed in groups. Riding the seas beside a group of fin whales intent on a meal requires caution. On a cool autumn day on the water, with winter almost in the air, the need to feed becomes urgent. Seven or eight slim, dark, 20-metre whales gulp their meals – which can include anything from krill to small schooling fish – and strain the water out through their baleen, then surface one by one, turning as they do, almost forming a circle.

Researchers Richard Sears, Martine Bérubé and their co-workers, as part of a blue whale research programme based on the north shore of Québec, have come to know some of the region's fin whales. The same in-

dividuals return to feed at the same time year after year, and researchers have been able to identify them by the light and dark marks and the scars on their heads, dorsal fins and backs.

One unique feature on each fin whale is a V-shaped area of light colouring, called a chevron, that extends from just behind the blowhole and sweeps back and down on both sides of the back. Yet the colour pattern is subtle, making it much more difficult to identify fin whales than it is to identify humpbacks, which have bold, easily recognizable tail patterns.

Fin whales are found throughout the world ocean, but most of the photo-identification research is being conducted off New England and in the Gulf of St. Lawrence. Researchers from various organizations contribute identification photographs and sighting information to the North Atlantic Finback Whale Catalog, which is based at College of the Atlantic, Bar Harbor, Maine.

FIN WHALE
(*Balaenoptera physalus*)
Size: 18.5 to 21.5 metres long, up to 26.8 metres and 45 tonnes.
Females slightly larger than males.
Calves at birth: About 6.5 metres and 2 tonnes.
Baleen: 260 to 480 plates on each side of the upper jaw. Plates grow up to 72 centimetres long.
Food: Fish, including sand lance, herring, capelin, pollack and cod, plus krill.
Habitat: Prefers deep water, but is also found close to shore.
Range: World ocean.
Status: Whaling has cut numbers from an estimated 548,000 to 120,000, about 20,000 of which are found in the northern hemisphere.

A fin whale, far left, cruises through the Sea of Cortés off Baja California, Mexico. Fin whales are the second largest animal on Earth; only blue whales are larger. As a fin whale moves through the water, spouting up to six metres high, it reveals a rolling back and a curved dorsal fin. Similar in appearance to the blue, it is smaller from head to tail.

The fin whale, left, displays one of the intriguing asymmetries of the natural world. The right lower jaw, including some of the baleen plates inside the mouth, is white; the other side of its head, as in other baleen whales, is black or grey. No one knows why this colouring occurs, but it may help to confuse the small-fish prey of fin whales.

Blue Whale

The big blue whale turned its spout on the sky, making a high-pressure geyser. As the oily spray drifted over the boat, cameras clicked. The mammoth animal drove forward, showing its broad, flat head, its fleshy splash guards protecting the two huge blowholes until the flaps closed. Then came the rolling back—rolling, rolling, still rolling, and then the 30-centimetre-high, curved dorsal fin. Finally, there was the tail, with the six-metre-wide flukes flipped high as the whale swam deep for its next assault on the krill population. It was Pita—a blue whale that had been a favourite for many seasons.

The researchers were in for a wet, somewhat dangerous roller-coaster ride. As the boat sped along through the choppy seas, rivers of water washed over the side, splashing cold into the boat. But Richard Sears and his team of researchers from the Mingan Island Cetacean Study in Québec remained intent. When blues were sighted, all comforts were sacrificed for the next 30 to 60 minutes. The goal? To take close-up photographs all along the back and on both sides of the whale for positive identification.

In the late 1970s, when Sears decided to study blue whales, many established scientists thought he was crazy. They did not think it was possible to take the kind of sharp photographs needed to identify and keep track of individuals. Sears has proved them wrong, although it has not been easy. He and his team work in the Gulf of St. Lawrence, where the blues come to feed from late spring through autumn. In small boats, the researchers fight rough seas, thick fogs and even snow at times to monitor the activities of these animals, which are ever on the move. And they have succeeded in cracking the blue whale identification code.

At the ocean's surface, the blue takes on the colour of the sea and sky. More than any other whale, it can reflect many shades of blue throughout the day. As sunset fades to twilight and night, the colour of the blue whale turns from shades of yellow to orange, red, lavender, dark grey and black. The reason is that it has a mottled back—a result of its uneven patterns of skin pigmentation.

The blue's colouring may help it avoid detection by the krill upon which it preys. But when it comes in

BLUE WHALE
(*Balaenoptera musculus*)

Size: 21.5 to 26.0 metres long, up to about 30.5 metres and 144 tonnes. Females slightly larger than males.

Calves at birth: About 7.0 metres long and 2.5 tonnes.

Baleen: 260 to 400 black plates on each side of the upper jaw. Plates grow up to about 90 centimetres long.

Food: Krill.

Habitat: Prefers deep water, but can be found close to shore.

Range: World ocean.

Status: Endangered. Whaling cut numbers from about 300,000 a century ago to an estimated 4,000 to 14,000 today. There may be fewer than 500 in the North Atlantic.

An adult blue surfaces, left, showing the distinctive mottling on its back that researchers use to identify individual blue whales and to give them names. Note the fleshy splash guards around the blowhole of this blue and the flipper barely visible underwater.

The north shore of the St. Lawrence River is one of the best places in the North Atlantic for krill, or euphausiids, the blue whale's food. Here, massive cold-water upwellings stir up nutrients in the water and provide food for the growing krill. The blue whales typically arrive as the krill become plentiful in early spring and stay through autumn until ice forces them to leave. They spend about eight months of the year eating as much and as often as they can.

to gulp a mouthful, the blue is so fast that camouflage may not even be necessary. Speed was the key feature that protected the blue whale until about a hundred years ago, when hunters obtained fast catcher boats and exploding harpoons. At that time, there may have been as many as 300,000 blues. Today, at most, there are only a few thousand left. Estimates range from 4,000 to 14,000.

Most blue whales appear to be loners on the feeding grounds. A big feeder needs space. Only the mothers and calves remain close to each other and then only during the first eight months, when the calf needs to nurse. Often, however, another blue is seen a kilometre or more away from a lone blue. Maybe blues, the largest animal on Earth, simply live life on a much bigger scale. Their low blasts carry easily for kilometres underwater. Perhaps they are all in close touch, or as close as they need to be, in a season when feeding is the main activity.

Humpback Whale

Scientist Jim Darling had no need of the headphones connected to the underwater microphone, or hydrophone: the sounds of humpbacks off Hawaii rumbled clearly through the bottom of the boat. One sounded like a herd of cattle lowing and someone practising a trumpet at the same time. The vibrations seemed almost to rattle the hull of the boat.

Here, for five winters in the late 1970s and early 1980s, a team of researchers led by Darling studied the behaviour of the humpback – an odd-looking, up-to-16-metre-long whale that both sings beautifully and is all grace in motion. A typical day started shortly after dawn, when land researchers using high-powered binoculars located surfacing whales and sent a radio message signalling the two research boats to investigate.

While the crew on one boat dropped a hydrophone into the water to record the sounds, the crew on the other tried to photograph the whale's tail to "get its ID." Then they would follow it and keep track of everything it did all day. Often, following an afternoon in the hot Hawaii sun, the researchers would be ready to go swimming; some swims became deep-diving attempts to observe and to determine the sex of the whales.

Like snowflakes, no two humpback tails are exactly alike. The photographs of their unique patterns are used to identify individual whales. Researchers have been able to confirm suspected migration-route patterns by matching tail photographs of whales seen off Hawaii with shots of those seen in summer near Alaska.

Over several winters in Hawaii, underwater photographs of the whales' genitals were taken to distinguish males from females. As it turned out, all the singers were males. When the singers weren't singing, they were fighting, a behaviour the researchers did not at first understand. In time, though, the true nature of the whales everyone had called "gentle giants" became clear. Watching closely, the researchers saw that all the rushing around was not simply in fun. Some whales smashed their tails against each other. Some drew blood. Although the wounds on the back, dorsal fin and head were superficial, it became clear that singing males were fighting for the chance to mate with a female.

HUMPBACK WHALE
(*Megaptera novaeangliae*)
Size: 11.5 to 13.0 metres long, up to 16.0 metres and about 35 tonnes. Females slightly larger than males.
Calves at birth: About 4.5 metres long and 1.5 tonnes.
Baleen: 270 to 400 plates on each side of the upper jaw. The mostly black plates each grow up to 70 centimetres long.
Food: Schooling fish, such as herring, sand lance, capelin, mackerel, cod and salmon, plus krill.
Habitat: Inshore and offshore waters; winter breeding and calving areas are close to shore.
Range: World ocean.
Status: Endangered. Whaling cut numbers from an estimated 115,000 to as few as about 10,000, of which 7,000 live in the northern hemisphere.

Note the bulging eyes on either side of the humpback whale's head, left, as it dives beneath the surface. The flippers—up to five metres long—are tucked against the animal's sides. Every humpback whale has bumps or knobs on its head that, when viewed close up, look like bolts on a piece of machinery. Yet the humpback in motion underwater is all grace—propelling itself by the up-and-down movement of its tail.

Arguably the most popular of all whales because of their playfulness, humpbacks are easy for whale watchers to identify and to get to know by name. This species may be the most-studied whale in research programmes that operate in every ocean from both ship and shore.

Northern Right Whale

The common names of the majority of whales were given to them by whalers, and generally, it is not difficult to understand the name's origin. The names blue and bowhead tell us what the whales look like. But the name for the northern right whale gives us no clue to its appearance. The "rightness" of the whale that launched the whaling industry in the 10th century was only in the eyes of those early hunters.

To a whaler, the "right" whale was the one that lived close to shore, was a slow swimmer and usually floated when dead. That was crucial to early whalers, who used small boats to hunt, kill and tow the animals to shore. But the rightness also had something to do with the catch itself: Once killed and landed, a single 45-tonne right whale would be rendered into 80 barrels of oil, to be used mainly as fuel for oil lamps. And the long, flexible baleen plates would be used to make umbrellas, corsets and other products.

By the early 16th century, few northern right whales remained in the eastern North Atlantic off the coast of Europe. European whalers, joined by early Americans, then started taking right whales in the rest of the Atlantic and, in the 1700s, in the Pacific. By the early 1900s, the northern right was thought to be nearly extinct. By then, whalers had equipped themselves with exploding harpoons and fast catcher boats and had turned to hunting other species.

In July 1980, researchers flying an aerial survey off the east coast of North America were delighted to rediscover a population of northern rights in the Bay of Fundy. In the weeks that followed, they found a total of 26 different rights, a number that included four mother-and-calf pairs. It was a surprising summer, full of hope for a nearly forgotten species, and it led to new research on the right whale.

Researchers Scott Kraus and Amy Knowlton, as well as other dedicated scientists from the New England Aquarium in Boston, Massachusetts, continue to study the northern right from Canada to Florida. To identify individuals, they photograph the distinctive callosities – hardened patches of skin – that are to be found on the head of every right whale.

Northern rights arrive on the sum-

mer feeding grounds off New England in April. Kraus, Knowlton and other researchers check new arrivals, at least some of which have swum up from Florida, taking photographs and meeting many old whale friends. Among them are always a few new calves. The whales "skim feed," swimming through the water with mouth open. Much more than other baleen whales, these mammals are food specialists. Although rights will sometimes eat krill, the main food of blues, their food of choice is copepods, tiny crustaceans less than 0.6 centimetres long; it takes about 8,000 copepods to fill a teaspoon. It takes millions to make a good mouthful for a whale – and a lot of swimming and filtering.

By early August, many northern right whales head for the Bay of Fundy, a feeding and nursery area preferred by mothers and calves. The whale researchers, too, bring their children and spend the summer and early autumn studying their subjects. Nearly 200 kilometres east of the Bay of Fundy, off Browns Bank south of Nova Scotia, other right whales gather to mate in what the researchers call "surface-active groups." These groups are mostly males pushing and shoving in an aggressive effort to mate with a female. But the female plays hard to get, lying on her back in the water. The male that can stay by her side the longest, waiting for her to roll over and take a breath, is the one that mates with her.

In November and December, female northern rights that are due to calve begin to migrate south along the coast to the waters off Florida and Georgia. In January, Kraus and Knowlton, flying south to meet the whales, count the new calves and try to identify the mothers. Kraus discovered the calving and mating grounds there in 1984. Since then, he has returned every year along with the whales. The whereabouts of all the other right whales during winter remains a mystery.

Fascinating to watch and special because of their rarity, northern rights are nonetheless slow, bulky, lumbering animals. Covered in callosities, whale lice and the odd facial hair, they are not the sort to win animal beauty contests. Right whale calves have no callosities and are almost slender when they are born. According to Kraus, "It's the only time in a right whale's life that it actually looks appealing."

NORTHERN RIGHT WHALE
(*Eubalaena glacialis*)
Size: 10.0 to 15.0 metres long, up to 17 metres and 63 tonnes. Females slightly larger than males.
Calves at birth: About 4.5 metres and 1 tonne.
Baleen: About 220 to 260 dark grey to black plates on each side of the upper jaw. Plates grow up to about 2.8 metres long.
Food: Mainly copepods; some krill.
Habitat: Prefers nearshore waters up to the edge of the continental shelf.
Range: North temperate zone. The southern right whale—almost identical in appearance—lives in the southern hemisphere.
Status: Endangered. Whaling has cut numbers from tens of thousands to only a few hundred. About 300 to 350 are left in the North Atlantic and perhaps 200 in the North Pacific.

The whitish areas on the northern right whale, left, are callosities—the right whale equivalent of horns on mountain sheep or rhinoceroses. These callosities often have hair growing out of them. Their whitish, sometimes pinkish, colour comes from tiny whale lice, called cyamids, that live on the whale without harming it and appear to feast on little pieces of whale skin. While the cyamids move around, each whale's callosity pattern stays fairly constant and can be used to identify a whale through its lifetime. The large callosity on the top of the head is called "the bonnet," a label given it by whalers.

Bowhead Whale

As the scientists huddled in a makeshift hut at the ice edge, trying to keep warm in the frigid Arctic spring, hundreds of bowhead whales swam by. For days, a blizzard had raged and no researcher had actually seen a bowhead – not the characteristic V-shaped blow or the bald black head with the white chin and the smooth, broad back. Yet they continued counting the whales as they passed.

The scientists' secret to monitoring the world of the whales was through underwater sound. When they are migrating, bowheads like to make sounds. The American researchers, Christopher W. Clark and his associates, had set up a series of hydrophones that with the aid of portable computers could pinpoint within eight kilometres where the bowheads were at any particular moment.

Most bowhead research has been aimed at answering the deceptively simple question of how many bowhead whales there are. Every spring for most of the past two decades, scientists have gathered by the ice edge near Point Barrow, Alaska's northernmost point, to watch and wait for bowheads to pass by. The autumn migration moves west and south to the open waters of the Bering Sea, while in spring, it passes back along the north coast of Alaska to the eastern Beaufort Sea. This is the largest concentration of bowheads in the world; smaller, separate populations are found across the eastern Canadian and Soviet Arctic.

Although bowheads are protected from commercial whaling by world-wide agreement, Inuit hunters have continued to take them at a rate of up to two or three dozen a year – a source of concern to some scientists, who until recently believed there to be fewer than 1,000 left in a population that, before whaling, numbered 20,000 to 30,000. The Inuit have said that the scientists were counting only the few which came close to shore during good weather and that there were, in fact, more like 5,000 bowheads. The sound studies conducted by Clark and his associates proved them right. There were, indeed, many more whales out there than could easily be seen. Even in the near-shore waters, visual spotters sometimes missed half the bowheads within the normal sighting range of about 2.5 kilometres. But noises of

BOWHEAD WHALE
(*Balaena mysticetus*)
Size: 14.0 to 17.5 metres long, up to 19.8 metres and 100 tonnes. Females slightly larger than males.
Calves at birth: About 4.0 to 4.5 metres.
Baleen: 230 to 360 dark grey or black plates on each side of the upper jaw. Plates grow up to 4.2 metres long.
Food: Copepods, krill and amphipods.
Habitat: Lives along the pack ice.
Range: Arctic Ocean.
Status: Endangered. Whaling has cut numbers from an estimated 30,000 to about 5,700 to 10,600 in the western Arctic, where most bowheads are found.

the passing bowheads carried regardless of weather and for distances underwater of eight kilometres or more. The latest estimates, based on sound and sightings, are that there are 5,700 to 10,600 bowhead whales in the western Arctic.

To researcher Clark, the bowhead sounds paint a vivid portrait of an animal that is surprisingly social. Travelling in groups of up to 15 animals widely spaced over an area of 10 to 20 square kilometres, bowheads seem to use their sounds to keep together and to communicate. Like foul-weather sailors or Arctic explorers, ever watching the sea and sky and listening for ice reports, the bowheads must stay tuned to danger. If they become trapped by fast-forming, unpredictable ice, they may be unable to reach the surface to breathe.

The ability to navigate through ice, according to Clark, requires skills that must be learned. Picture a group of whales, each member investigating leads in the ice and then communicating its findings to the others. Although bowheads can make intensely loud noises, they tend to produce sounds at a level that is moderate yet loud enough to be heard by every whale in the immediate travelling group.

There is no proof that bowheads echolocate in an advanced way as do some toothed whales and dolphins, which can obtain precise sound pictures of their underwater world. Yet Clark and his associate William Ellison believe that the bowheads could be listening to the echoes of their own sounds off the ice. That would give the migrating bowhead a general idea of where the ice-free paths might be. Indeed, bowheads have been seen apparently navigating their way through huge ice floes, turning to swim around them well before the floes come into view.

Similar in appearance to the northern right whale but without callosities, a bowhead, left, surfaces in early summer at the edge of an ice floe in Lancaster Sound near Baffin Island. According to observers, the lone male repeatedly dived under the ice to feed, surfacing each time at this spot.

Like belugas and narwhals, bowheads are ruled by the forming, moving and thawing of ice. The ice and the often difficult weather conditions also present obstacles to the development of oil and gas resources in the Arctic. Although oil companies believe they can transport oil safely, the Alaskan oil spill of the *Exxon Valdez* in March 1989 gives us an idea of the long-lasting environmental damage that can be done by a big oil spill in the Arctic.

Toothed Whales   Sperm Whale

Imagine a big male sperm whale preparing to make a deep dive. Resting at the surface, it spouts 50 or 60 times, about once every 15 seconds, before lifting its broad, triangular tail flukes and heading down – a hundred metres, two hundred, three, four, a kilometre or more into the black.

As it slips beneath the surface of the sea, a sperm whale probably regulates its buoyancy, in part, by cooling or heating the huge reservoir of clear liquid oil, called spermaceti, that is inside its head. This high-quality oil is the main reason humans have hunted the sperm whale. But for a mammal that roams the deep sea in search of food, a big head full of spermaceti has other uses. Scientists speculate that taking in water through the blowhole helps the whale cool the oil and

change it into wax, making its body heavier. Pumping blood around the spermaceti, on the other hand, liquefies the oil and makes the whale more buoyant.

The sperm whale's head is the biggest in the animal kingdom. Up to 18 metres long, a mature male sperm whale has a head that takes up almost a third of its body length, or about 5 metres. Its high forehead protrudes more than a metre over its long, narrow lower jaw, which, when closed, almost disappears. But when open, the sperm whale's mouth strikes a menacing pose: the lower jaw has two nearly parallel rows of sharp, widely spaced teeth that fit neatly into the holes, or sockets, of the upper jaw when the mouth is shut.

To enable it to hunt in dark ocean

canyons, the sperm whale sends clicking sounds to help it locate its favourite food – squid. The clicks, which are directed through the case containing the spermaceti, travel through the water and bounce off objects in the whale's path. By reading the reflected echoes, whales can "see" their way to the squid.

The battles between giant squid and sperm whales in the ocean canyons have never been witnessed by humans, but the disc-shaped sucker marks found on sperm whales are evidence of the scars of battle. There are various species of squid, averaging about 1.4 kilograms, although the elusive giant squid can grow up to 20 metres long. The sperm whale kills the squid by grasping it with its teeth and swallowing it ten-

tacle by tentacle. Every day, a mature male sperm whale eats more than 1,300 kilograms of food – about a thousand squid.

Sperm whales live in various kinds of groups, depending on their age and sex. Mothers with calves and juveniles stay together in what are called "nursery schools." When a mother gets hungry and needs to dive deep in search of food, she is able to leave her youngster at the surface in the temporary care of another female.

The females trade off the baby-sitting arrangements.

Although humans have spent centuries whaling, scientists are only beginning to get to know the real sperm whale in its own world. More than one scientist has suggested that the sperm whale may be the poet of the sea, its large brain storing long oral histories and its odd sounds the sea's epic poems. It may be many years before the secrets of this giant brain are revealed.

SPERM WHALE
(Physeter macrocephalus)
Size: Females up to 12.0 metres long and 18 tonnes.
Males up to 18 metres long and about 63 tonnes.
Calves at birth: About 4 metres and 1 tonne.
Teeth: 18 to 25 teeth on each side of the lower jaw.
Food: Mainly squid, with some fish and octopus.
Habitat: Throughout the deep ocean, especially in canyons at the edge of the continental shelf.
Range: World ocean. Females with young prefer tropical seas; males range well into polar waters.
Status: Whaling has cut numbers a little in many areas, yet the species is not endangered. The world population is in the hundreds of thousands.

The large block head and the prunelike skin are immediately recognizable physical characteristics of the adult sperm whale, left. When a sperm whale dives, the relatively small flippers tuck into its sides.

Sperm whales travel far from shore in search of squid in water that ranges from hundreds of metres to a kilometre or more deep. Unable to see, the whales use sonar clicks to find the squid—and then the battle begins. A favourite food is the giant squid.

Pygmy & Dwarf Sperm Whales

In the temperate and tropical seas of the world ocean live small, rare sperm whales. Related to the giant sperm whale, these pygmy and dwarf sperms feed mainly on squid off the continental shelf. They have rarely been observed at sea by research teams, but they are often found stranded, or washed ashore, year-round on the east and west coasts of the United States. Some have been found alive and rushed to aquariums where they have died a few days or weeks later.

The few sightings of these whales in the wild have revealed slow-moving, shy animals that travel in groups of two or three and up to seven at the most. In calm seas, the dwarf and pygmy sperm whales have been seen basking on the water's surface. With their conical snouts and the gill-like crescent marks on their cheeks, they are often mistaken for sharks. So little is known about dwarf and pygmy sperms that scientists have been unable to tell them apart from their behaviour. As a consequence, many records of the two species – sightings as well as strandings and catch statistics – are muddled.

The dwarf sperm whale is indeed closely related to the pygmy sperm whale, though smaller, with a shorter, blunter snout. The dwarf sperm has a larger dorsal fin than the pygmy sperm has, and it is positioned farther forward, close to the centre of its back. Its dolphinlike dorsal fin sometimes causes the dwarf sperm whale, seen in the photograph, right, to be mistaken for a dolphin.

PYGMY SPERM WHALE
(Kogia breviceps)
Size: 2.5 to 3.0 metres long, up to 3.5 metres and 400 kilograms.
Calves at birth: About 1.2 metres.
Teeth: 10 to 16 in each lower jaw; none in upper jaws.
Food: Squid, deepwater fish, crabs and shrimps.
Habitat: Prefers open ocean in tropical and warm temperate waters.
Range: World ocean.
Status: Unknown. Fairly uncommon.

DWARF SPERM WHALE
(*Kogia simus*)
Size: 2.0 to 2.5 metres long, up to 2.7 metres and 272 kilograms.
Calves at birth: About 1 metre.
Teeth: 7 to 12 (up to 13) in each lower jaw; 0 to 3 in each upper jaw.
Food: Squid, deepwater fish.
Habitat: Prefers open ocean in tropical and warm temperate waters.
Range: World ocean.
Status: Unknown. Fairly uncommon.

Beaked Whales

Beaked whales are a group of primitive-looking whales, some 19 species in all, found in the deep ocean. Small to medium in size compared with other whale species, they have prominent beaks, short flippers, two V-shaped grooves on their throats and short tail flukes with no middle notch. Although several beaked species – especially Cuvier's beaked whale, Baird's beaked whale (seen below) and the northern bottlenose whale – have been caught by whalers, most of the others are rare. Their rarity is partly due to the secret lives they lead in small groups far out at sea. Only a few scientists have ever seen one alive; those who have got only a fleeting glimpse as the mammal dived deep and disappeared.

The only real opportunity scientists have to study beaked whales occurs when they are washed ashore, usually dead. Most of what we know about them is based on these infrequent strandings. In 1972, soon after he had joined the Smithsonian Institution as a curator of mammals, James G. Mead found a live juvenile male Baird's beaked whale stranded on the New Jersey coast. Transported to the New York Aquarium, it died within 24 hours. It would be one of the few beaked whales he would ever see alive.

Studying beaked whales is detective work. In 1976, Mead and fellow scientist Robert L. Brownell Jr. found the skull of a new small species on a beach in Peru; it had been caught by a fisherman. In the years since that incident, a few other bones have washed ashore there – enough to allow a brief scientific description and designation as a new species.

Northern Bottlenose Whale

With clues pieced together from strandings, scientists are starting to deduce how beaked whales live in the wild. Mead believes they attain sexual maturity late and live to ages that approach the human life span. Since beaked whales usually strand alone or in pairs, they may live in small groups, perhaps three to five individuals at most.

The best way to identify the species is to look at their teeth. Generally, only the males have them – two to four in all, usually in the lower jaw. The teeth often stick out on the sides of the jaw and have barnacles growing on them. One beaked whale – the straptoothed whale from the southern hemisphere – has two teeth that look more like tusks growing out and around the upper jaw, restricting the mouth opening. These large teeth may be of limited use for catching their main food, which is squid.

The teeth in male beaked whales appear to be a sexual characteristic, like the tusk of the narwhal or the song of the humpback. Many males are covered with scratches and scars, which tell of fights between males of the same species far below the surface. Perhaps the whale with the biggest or sharpest teeth is the one that has the first chance of mating.

On the following pages, we will meet several of the better-known beaked whales. The background files are sometimes sketchy, and the illustrations are based on whales found stranded on beaches, since it has been impossible to photograph some in the wild.

NORTHERN BOTTLENOSE WHALE
(*Hyperoodon ampullatus*)
Size: Males up to 9.8 metres long and 7 tonnes.
Females up to 8 metres long. Males much larger than females.
Calves at birth: About 3.5 metres.
Teeth: 1 on each side near tip of lower jaw, found only in males.
Food: Mainly squid, plus herring and bottom invertebrates.
Habitat: Deep polar and cooler temperate waters off the continental shelf.
Range: North Atlantic Ocean.
Status: Unknown. Whaling has reduced numbers.

CUVIER'S BEAKED WHALE
(*Ziphius cavirostris*)
Size: Females 6 to 7 metres long, up to 7.5 metres.
Males 5.5 to 6.5 metres long. Females slightly larger than males.
Calves at birth: About 2.7 metres.
Teeth: 1 on each side of lower jaw, usually found only in mature males.
Food: Squid and deepwater fish.
Habitat: Offshore in tropical and temperate waters.
Range: World ocean.
Status: Unknown.

BAIRD'S BEAKED WHALE
(*Berardius bairdii*)
Size: Females up to 12.8 metres long and 13.5 tonnes.
Males up to 11.8 metres long. Females slightly larger than males.
Calves at birth: About 4.5 metres.
Teeth: Usually 2 on each side at tip of lower jaw in males and females. Teeth protrude when mouth is closed.
Food: Squid, octopus, deep-sea fishes and crustaceans.
Habitat: Prefers deep temperate waters.
Range: North Pacific Ocean.
Status: Unknown, but may have been reduced by whaling.

Blainville's Beaked Whale, Hubbs' Beaked Whale

BLAINVILLE'S BEAKED WHALE
(*Mesoplodon densirostris*)
Size: Up to 4.7 metres long and about 3 tonnes.
Teeth: 1 large tooth on each side of raised lower jaw.
Food: Squid.
Habitat: Prefers deep tropical to cool temperate waters off the continental shelf.
Range: World ocean.
Status: Unknown, but may be commonest beaked whale.

HUBBS' BEAKED WHALE
(*Mesoplodon carlhubbsi*)
Size: Up to 5.3 metres long and 1.5 tonnes.
Calves at birth: Probably close to 2.5 metres.
Teeth: 1 on each side of lower jaw.
Food: Squid and deepwater fishes.
Habitat: Offshore cold temperate waters.
Range: North Atlantic Ocean.
Status: Unknown.

Narwhal

In the low light of evening in the high Canadian Arctic off Baffin Island, scientist John K.B. Ford witnessed a bizarre, yet apparently common and even ancient ritual. Male narwhals had gathered at the surface of the smooth waters of the bay. As they raised their tusks out of the water at a sharp angle, they began crossing, almost intertwining them with those of other males.

Scientists suspect that the narwhal's tusk functions like the antlers of a deer or a mountain goat: the longest tusks or antlers are on the largest animals and can therefore be used as visual cues of size; the animal with the largest tusk wins the first chance to mate. One scientist has suggested that narwhals may line up, tusk to tusk, to see whose tusk is longest. Per-

haps a blast of sound, vibrating along the tusk of the larger animal, helps make the point.

If neither animal is significantly larger than the other, a tusk fight may occur. The incidents of tusk crossings may be a prelude to the competition between males for females. Indeed, the heads of most male narwhals are covered with scars, probably from a combination of fighting, playing and accident.

Closely related to belugas, narwhals are also known for the varied sounds they produce. Ford has recorded them at length and has found that narwhals seem to make signature sounds — sounds that are unique to each individual. While more scientific work needs to be done, it might be possible to use the sounds to iden-

tify and survey a population. Narwhals also make clicks, probably for echolocation.

Recent narwhal studies have tried to answer two main questions. The first is whether Inuit hunting in the eastern Canadian and Greenland Arctic is hurting the species. Narwhal population estimates in summer range from 25,000 to 35,000 for Canada and Greenland, probably enough to sustain the number of animals taken (including those killed but not harvested)—about 1,000 a year. In any case, it is important for the hunt to be closely monitored and controlled.

The second question is whether oil can be safely transported through the Arctic waterways, and the answer is far more conclusive: the catastrophic effect of an oil spill in the Arctic was only hinted at by the *Exxon Valdez* incident of March 1989, when 40 million litres of crude oil spilled into the waters off Alaska, killing numerous birds and marine mammals. Such a spill in the eastern Canadian Arctic would be disastrous for narwhals and for all life for many years to come.

NARWHAL
(*Monodon monoceros*)
Size: Up to 5 metres long (not including tusk) and about 1.6 tonnes. Males slightly larger than females.
Calves at birth: About 1.5 metres and 80 kilograms.
Teeth: None in mouth, 2 adult teeth in gum of upper jaw; in the male, the left tooth erupts through the upper lip at age 1, reaching 3 metres or more and weighing up to 10 kilograms.
Food: Squid, polar cod, bottom fish such as Greenland halibut, shrimps and crabs.
Habitat: Deep water, for much of the year near the ice.
Range: Arctic Ocean, especially high Arctic.
Status: Population unknown, but best estimate is 25,000 to 50,000. May be declining in some areas because of hunting.

A narwhal in Eclipse Sound, at the northern end of Baffin Island in the Canadian Arctic, raises its tusk out of the water, top far left. Actually a tooth that appears in young males at about 1 year of age, the tusk pierces the upper lip and spirals as it grows to a length of up to three metres. It is made of pulp tissue and is hollow inside. In older males, the tusk is brittle and breaks easily; about one in three male narwhals has a broken tusk.

A group of male narwhals swims together in Canada's high Arctic, left, their tusks just visible below the surface. There are many theories about the use of the tusk; it may be a weapon or a tool to open breathing holes in the ice or to catch food, but the best explanation seems to be that the tusk gives the narwhal status at mating time. In rare cases, animals with two tusks have been found.

Beluga

When beluga researcher Pierre Béland was a child growing up in the province of Québec, his mother would point to the rounded white forms of belugas passing in the St. Lawrence River. Béland was never sure they were real.

White slivers momentarily visible on the sea, the belugas could have been pieces of ice, whitecaps or a shimmering mirage. Slipping by, these small, ghostlike whales were full of mystery. But if they were whales, wondered Béland, what were they doing in a river?

Belugas live in the Arctic waters of Canada, the United States and the Soviet Union. Most spend a large part of their year near the edge of the advancing and retreating ice pack. In summer, some ascend rivers for hundreds of kilometres, feeding on fish. The St. Lawrence River, the most southerly habitat for belugas, was once an Arctic sea – home to Arctic seals, narwhals and bowhead whales. When the ice from the last glaciation receded about 10,000 years ago, the St. Lawrence belugas stayed and survived as a separate population.

In the autumn of 1982, Béland and fellow researcher Daniel Martineau finally saw their first St. Lawrence beluga close up. It had died at sea and washed ashore. Since then, their mission has been to preserve the living belugas by studying the dead. The pair have recorded more than 75 dead belugas and have sampled or autopsied many of them, including some stillborn calves. They have found 24 different potentially toxic contaminants in beluga tissues and organs in concentrations that are among the highest in all marine mammals. The pollution comes from aluminum and other industrial plants located upriver from where the belugas live. Some of the animals have cancerous tumours and sores, and others have suppressed immune systems – a breakdown in the body's defence against disease that is often attributed to contaminants such as PCBs and DDT.

Today, the St. Lawrence belugas number between 450 and 500 – down from an estimated 5,000 in the year 1900. Although pollution cannot be proved to be the cause of the whales' decline – dams and hunting have also contributed – it appears to be playing a major role. Belugas and other whales need clean food and clean water. Peo-

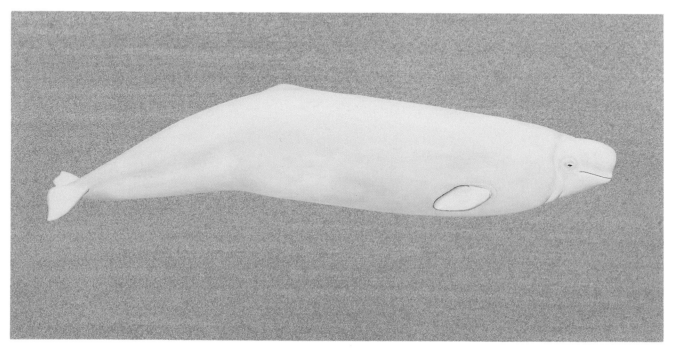

ple living in the vast area of Canada and the United States that is drained by the St. Lawrence River are beginning to recognize the threats to all life from polluted water, but the problem is enormous. It will be very costly to stop all industries from pouring their waste into rivers, yet that is what must be done in order to protect the whales and other animals. The beluga population in the Arctic remains healthy, but the time may one day come when children growing up along the St. Lawrence River will neither see white whales in the distance nor even stop to wonder about them.

BELUGA
(*Delphinapterus leucas*)
Size: 3 to 5 metres long, up to 4.5 metres and about 1.5 tonnes. Males slightly larger than females.
Calves at birth: About 1.5 metres.
Teeth: Up to 11 teeth in each side of upper and lower jaw, at least 32 total.
Food: Fish, including char, sand lance, capelin, pollack, cod and salmon, plus shrimp and octopus.
Habitat: Prefers shallow waters, rivers and estuaries.
Range: Arctic Ocean, although extends into North Pacific and North Atlantic, including the St. Lawrence River.
Status: World population unknown but probably 40,000 to 55,000. May be declining in some areas because of hunting and pollution.

Like many toothed whales, belugas, left, are curious predators—always on the lookout for fish and other prey to supplement their diet. Their smooth all-white bodies and lack of a dorsal fin make them an easy species to identify at sea. Wherever they go, the sea becomes alive with their screams, whistles and other sounds. Belugas also have an ability rare among whales: they can turn their heads from side to side and look over—or under—their shoulders. Along with their Arctic camouflage colouring, their head-turning ability may help them to feed or to avoid predators such as polar bears and killer whales.

The size and shape of a whale's head, teeth and baleen provide clues to the animal's feeding habits. A northern right whale, with its huge head and long baleen, feeds on small organisms called copepods. It swims steadily through the water, mouth open, filtering its food. The fast-moving blue whale, with its slim head and great expanding pouch, gulps krill. A single mouthful may contain up to 45 tonnes of food and water; a blue whale needs to ingest about four or more tonnes of krill in a single day.

Toothed species, such as sperm and beaked whales, on the other hand, use their teeth for grasping prey, mainly squid and fish. They do not chew, but their large throats enable them to swallow food items whole.

Krill, or euphausiids, facing page, top left, are several species of shrimplike crustaceans that live in cold waters and range in size from less than 0.6 centimetres to more than 6.0 centimetres.

The preferred food of sperm and beaked whales, as well as of certain dolphins, squid, facing page, top right, range in size from a few centimetres to more than 13 metres long. A whole 12-metre giant squid was once recovered from the stomach of a sperm whale.

Several types of feeding techniques are illustrated on the facing page, bottom. The humpback, left, with its throat pleats expanded, moves to the surface to scoop up a school of tiny fish; the northern right, top right, a skim feeder, eats on the run, taking in a meal of copepods; the sperm, middle right, chases down a good-sized squid; and a gray whale, bottom left, grubs along the bottom for food.

A humpback whale, top, opens its mouth following a surge to the surface, draining out all the water. The swirls of water at the surface come from the "bubble net" that humpbacks make. When humpbacks blow streams of bubbles, the bubbles rise to the surface and form a net that confuses schools of fish and traps them inside. Seconds later, the whale swims up through the bubbles with its mouth open, gulping the fish.

Gray whales, with their short, thick jaws and short baleen plates, often grub on or near the muddy bottom, sucking up small organisms. Some feed on one side only, and the baleen plates on that side are usually worn shorter than those on the other side. Seen from the surface, bottom, a gray whale stirs up the sediments and leaves dirty trails wherever it goes.

Fighting & Playing

Until recently, scientists and whale watchers have thought of whales as "gentle giants." Aggressive behaviour between whales, although rarely witnessed, was thought of as play. But since the late 1970s, when scientists began to spend long days out in small boats close to the animals, their view of some species has changed.

On the tropical breeding grounds, a male humpback whale often accompanies a female and calf as an "escort," a role apparently assumed by a male that hopes to mate with the female. When another male approaches a female or her escort, the escort blows streams of bubbles in a screen that serves not only to block the view but also to act as a warning signal. If the other male refuses to back off, the escort lashes his tail in the face or on the back of the intruder or rams him broadside. The sound of whales ramming each other underwater, recorded on hydrophones, has been compared to the sound of two huge sacks of glass being smashed together. These crashes and tail lashes often draw blood as the sharp barnacles on the attacking whale tear at the other's skin and blubber layer. Such wounds, although not serious, reveal the intensity of the encounter.

Male right whales on the mating grounds push and butt each other to get close to a female, but they do not seem to be as violent as humpbacks. Male sperm whales are known to rake their teeth along one another's backs in what is thought to be a competition for the position of master of a group of females, with exclusive mating privileges. A female right whale, on the other hand, appears to mate with many males in one season.

Male narwhals have been seen using their tusks in jousting contests, sparring to assert dominance. Rarely, the tusk punctures the skin or even kills another narwhal.

Yet when whales fight, the injuries seem mostly superficial. Although it would be easy for 35-tonne whales to hurt each other, they do not. Instead, one of the males yields. On another day, in another contest, the losing male may have another chance to win a female and, through mating, to pass his genes on to the next generation. In this way, the species stays strong, because only the fittest males are able to breed.

A group of Baird's beaked whales of various ages—3 of 12 visible at the surface—swims through Monterey Bay, California, far left. The group spouted together, lying at the surface and resting before diving again. Note the scratches on the back of the animal in the foreground. Only the males of various beaked whale species have teeth, and they apparently get the scratches on their backs from the teeth of other males of the same species. Such marks tell of playful or aggressive encounters; the males may be competing for females.

Duelling narwhals, left, meet in Eclipse Sound near Pond Inlet, Baffin Island, in the Canadian Arctic. The back of a third male, probably in retreat, can be seen almost between the tusks. Male narwhals appear to use their distinctive tusk when competing for females. The head region around the tusk is often scarred, and heavily scarred narwhals often have broken tusks, apparently from battles. One scientist suggests that the tusk crossing might be an attempt to line up the tusks to see which animal has the best—longest or strongest—tusk. The winner may earn the chance to mate with a female. Since the tusks appear to figure in sexual status, they are probably not used to break ice or to spear fish or other food. No narwhal would want to risk breaking his status symbol except in the heat of battle.

The Singing of Whales

Millions of years before the first humans walked on Earth, the sounds of whales filled every sea. Early sailors, lying in their bunks at night, heard the sounds through the hulls of their ships. By the late 1960s, scientists had begun to record the sounds and had discovered that at least one species, the humpback, was actually singing songs. Since then, researchers have studied humpbacks to try to determine why they make sounds in such orderly and beautiful patterns. The findings are stripping away the mystery of the songs, although much remains to be learned.

A humpback song lasts 6 to 35 minutes and may then be repeated. Sometimes a song session lasts an hour, sometimes for many hours; 22 hours is the longest session ever recorded. The sounds cover roughly the range found on a piano: seven octaves. There are at least 20 different syllables, or notes, each sounded as a chirp, cry or moan. A group of syllables makes up a phrase, and a group of phrases, which may be repeated any number of times, is called a theme. Six themes make up the average song. Some themes of the song may have low, rumbling choruses; others have high sounds like trumpet blasts in melodies, which are repeated and elaborated.

Only the males sing, and most of their singing takes place on the shallow mating and calving grounds in the Tropics. Research in the late 1970s revealed that within a breeding ground, all humpbacks sing the same song, although each individual has its own way of singing. Over time, the song slowly changes, and all the whales keep up with the latest version. The differences are slight during a season, but after eight years, the song is completely different. This places humpbacks somewhere between birds and humans—the songs of certain birds change slightly

because of mimicry of new sounds, and humans can make up entirely new songs.

While no one knows exactly why humpback whales sing, scientists believe the songs probably figure in mating. Rather than attracting females, the songs seem intended to announce that the males are available. Perhaps the best singer gets the first chance to mate. Often, however, when a singer approaches a mother-calf pair, he has to fight another male that is acting as an escort. Both stop singing, and the winner of the battle stays with the female. The other male resumes singing until he is ready to make another challenge.

Marine zoologist John K.B. Ford, top far left, has studied the sounds of several species of whales and dolphins. His work at the University of British Columbia led to the discovery of dialects in killer whale schools. Since then, working for the West Coast Whale Research Foundation and based at the Vancouver Public Aquarium, Ford has recorded the sounds of narwhals and belugas and has analyzed them by means of sonograms, which are visual printouts of the sounds. Like a piece of written music, sonograms show the frequency, or pitch.

Ford makes his recordings from boat or shore. A hydrophone picks up the sounds, bottom far left, and a cable leads to a tape recorder. The sounds of toothed whale species include clicks used for echolocation and a wide variety of whistles and screams, some of which appear to be sounds that the whale is using to communicate.

Compared with toothed whales, baleen whales use sound in very different ways. Humpbacks, for example, sing songs. The male humpback, left, somewhere off Maui in the Hawaiian Islands, assumes the classic singing pose. With his head pointing down at a 45-degree angle, the whale stays 16 metres or more underwater while he is singing. Each time he surfaces, it is during the same part of the song. A song session may last up to 22 hours, with only brief interruptions when the whale surfaces for air.

Scientist Roger Payne, with Scott McVay, discovered the humpback songs in the late 1960s. In 1970, they released a best-selling record of the singing humpbacks. Katy Payne and other scientists continue to study the songs today.

Like humans, whales are social mammals. They live in groups of various sizes, some arranged by sex or age. Sometimes, these groups form for only part of the year. Some travel together to help one another find food or to fend off predators such as sharks or killer whales. Others, like the humpbacks, are brought together by the allure of the mating-ground rituals: singing, competing and mating.

What constitutes a whale group? To human observers, individual whales may seem to be arranged too loosely to be part of a group. Yet there are periods in the year, if not every day, when these individuals are within close touching distance of other whales.

Social behaviour varies widely from one species to the next. The toothed whales tend to travel in large, long-term groups in which some or most of the individuals stay together year after year. Sperm whales form various types of schools, or stable groups: young bachelor males (bachelor school); mature males (bull school); juveniles of both sexes (juvenile school); adult females with calves and juveniles of both sexes (nursery school); adult females with calves and juveniles joined by an adult male during the breeding season (harem school); and lone adult males.

The best-studied sperm whale groups have been nursery schools of about 20 whales. Seven individuals identified one year in a school in the Indian Ocean were seen together the following year in the same area. And some of the adult females from another nursery school remained together for more than 10 years.

Scientists believe that baleen whales are less group-oriented because of the way they feed on tiny organisms. The amount of food each whale needs every day probably requires widely spaced positions on the feeding grounds. Yet bowheads, rights, humpbacks and fins are sometimes seen in tens or even in hundreds, perhaps temporary groups in a particularly rich krill or copepod patch. Later the same day, or the following day, at least for gray, humpback and right whales, the same individuals may be seen alone or forming other groups.

Although baleen whales seem to exhibit less loyalty than do the toothed whales, all experience that most basic and universal bond common to social mammals – the tie between mother and offspring.

At birth, baby whales, like most mammals, are helpless. Many are pushed to the surface for their first breath of air – either by their mother or by another whale on the scene to assist the mother. Newborn calves often have wrinkled skin, and the dorsal fin may be folded over, lifting only after the youngster spends a few days in the world. The babies start swimming right away, but most females bear their calves in warm or sheltered waters so that the youngster does not lose valuable calories trying to keep warm. The calf stays close to its mother to nurse, feeding every few hours by placing its mouth against the underside of her belly, where the teats are concealed.

With most whales, the mother-calf relationship lasts only a year or two. During this time, the youngsters are gradually moulded into social creatures. Staying close to their mothers, they learn how to feed, play, vocalize and avoid predators. The early sustained intimacy of all social mammals is what drives them to seek close bonds with others of their kind for the rest of their lives.

On the warm winter calving grounds, far left, a right whale calf stays close to its female parent. The calf is completely dependent upon its mother for milk and protection and probably learns from her most of what it needs to know to survive.

After giving birth and nursing, the mother is hungry. Within four months of giving birth, right whales depart the tropical calving grounds and head for the cold-water feeding grounds, 1,500 to 2,000 kilometres away. The calf travels beside or behind the mother, nursing from time to time as they migrate.

A humpback whale, left, smacks its tail at the surface, an activity known as tail lobbing. Such playful behaviour is typically seen in immature whales. Often it is a young animal seeking to imitate its parents for no other reason but fun. For all whale youngsters, as for other social mammals, playing helps an animal learn the actions of adults — some of which may be crucial for survival. Tail lobbing may be a way for an adult toothed whale to herd fish. The same action may also be an aggressive gesture by humpback males in battle. Then, it is known as tail lashing.

Whaling & the Status of Whales

For most of recorded history, humans have gone to sea in search of the whale. Some have needed food or oil; some have had a taste for adventure. Others have been greedy for the riches that often came from a successful voyage.

The first people known to make use of whales were from the Arctic. At least 5,000 years ago, early hunters and gatherers began cutting up whales that were stranded on the shores of northern Canada, Alaska and Norway; it is not hard to see why it was impossible to ignore such a large package of food and oil. In time, these people came to rely on whales and took the next step – they went out to sea to kill them or to try to drive them inshore. In Norway, according to rock carvings dating to 2200 B.C., humans even hunted whales from a canoe – probably the slow-moving northern right whales that often swam close to land.

In fact, northern right whales were the first to be threatened by too much whaling. In the 11th century, the Basques, who lived in what are now Spain and France, began hunting right whales off western Europe. As local populations disappeared, the hunters moved north to Norway and the Arctic. By the 1600s, the Basques were joined in the Arctic by the Dutch, British, French and Germans. They began moving west to Iceland, Greenland and, by the late 1500s, to North America. Sailing on ships 30 metres long or more, with crews of 30 to 50 men, they would sometimes stay at sea longer than a year. Rights and bowheads were the main quarry, followed by humpbacks.

Whaling was tough work, and the long voyages were exhausting and dangerous. Some lost their lives during storms at sea, and a few were killed by an angry whale struggling with a harpoon in its back. Yet many whalers grew ambitious and were eager to sail in search of new frontiers.

As Europeans sailed far and wide, early American colonists joined the hunt. The era of American whaling lasted from the late 1600s to the 1900s. Setting out from New England ports, American whalers scoured the North Atlantic and the Arctic and then ventured to the South Atlantic before turning to the vast Pacific, setting up bases in Hawaii.

Fuelled by the continuing demand for oil, as well as for baleen, which was used in umbrellas and corsets, whaling had by the late 1800s led to the serious decline of all the big, slow-swimming cetaceans – bowhead, right and gray whales, as well as the slightly faster humpbacks. Whalers were running out of animals they could readily catch. But three developments changed all that.

The first was the invention of the explosive-grenade harpoon, complete with cannon and mount for the bow of a ship. The second was the development of faster steam-driven ships to replace sailing ships. These two advances made it possible for hunters to catch the faster blue, fin and sei species. The third development was the opening of the Antarctic – the richest whale grounds in the world. For the first two decades of the 1900s, whaling in the Antarctic was land-based. In 1925, factory ships, which made it possible for whalers to process the large mammals at sea, further extended their reach. Blues were captured until whalers could find no more. Then they turned to the next largest, fin whales, and finally to sei whales, eliminating nearly all of each species in turn. As with the rights, grays and bowheads before them, they, too, were driven to commercial extinction – the point at which there are so few members of a species that it becomes too difficult and costly to find them.

As whale populations dwindled in the late 1940s, several countries set up an organization to manage them – the International Whaling Commission (IWC). Its goal was to enable the whales to recover and then to keep them at a level that would allow

whalers to continue hunting them indefinitely. But the quotas set by the IWC were based on a poor understanding of whale biology. The allowable catches were far too large, and populations continued to decline.

In the 1970s, however, with most of the world's whale species reduced in number, the IWC began to work on a commercial moratorium. Several nonwhaling countries joined and, together with former whaling countries such as the United States and Canada, stopped the industry. In 1982, for the first time, zero quotas for all species were adopted as part of the moratorium to go into effect in 1986, although a few countries have refused to honour the ban. Under the cover of science, Japan, Iceland and Norway have continued to catch a few hundred minke, fin and sei whales each year, supposedly to be used for research. The Japanese still consider whale meat a delicacy and grind up the bones for fertilizer. Japan

remains the main market for whales caught anywhere in the world.

Some hunting of bowheads, narwhals and belugas continues on a small scale in the United States, Canada, the Soviet Union and a few other countries by Inuit and other natives. Such whaling is regulated by each country but is overseen by the IWC.

Hundreds of books have been written about whaling–from academic accounts to stirring novels such as *Moby-Dick; or the Whale* by Herman Melville. But for the great whales, whaling was all bad news. While no species became extinct, several species, especially the northern right and the blue, were reduced to such low numbers that they may never recover. The ocean, filled with hundreds of thousands more whales than we see today, was once a much more interesting place. If, indeed, several large species do become extinct, it will be a sad last chapter in the story of whales and humans.

A whaler, far left, lances a harpooned sperm whale, attempting to secure it to his boat. In the Azores–a group of islands 1,000 kilometres west of Portugal in the North Atlantic–whalers continue their primitive whaling from small boats with hand-held harpoons. Before the invention of the exploding harpoon gun and the development of steam-driven ships, this was the common method of whaling.

Rubble and memories are all that remain of an abandoned whaling station, left, at Williamsport, Newfoundland, closed in 1972. With the invention of the harpoon gun in the 1860s, Norwegians, who had whaled first off Norway, moved to North America and built whaling stations in places such as Newfoundland, British Columbia, Québec and Nova Scotia. Whales provided the oil that fuelled homes and industry. The oil could also be turned into soap, lipstick, candles, lubricants, crayons, margarine and many other products. Whale baleen was turned into such things as umbrellas and ladies' corsets. With such an easily exploitable source of wealth, humans predictably became greedy. The whalers of the 19th and 20th centuries succeeded in killing more than 90 percent of most large whale species –until there were so few by the early 1970s that most countries stopped whaling. Meanwhile, cheaper oils and other substitutes, often from plants or synthetic sources, have been found for all the products that whales once supplied.

The era of commercial whaling in Canada continued until 1972. Since then, only Inuit people have hunted whales in Canadian waters, taking a limited number of bowhead whales, belugas and narwhals.

Whale Watching

The thrill of coming close to these extremely large, intelligent and apparently friendly wild animals at sea is hard to explain. But since most whaling came to an end in the early 1970s, whale watching – a completely new way of looking at the animals – has become incredibly popular. Rather than undertaking journeys in order to kill whales, people are going out in boats to meet them. All along the east and west coasts of North America, millions of schoolchildren have already been sprayed or splashed by whales, and some children are going back and getting to know individuals by name.

People who do not happen to live close to the sea are encouraged to visit these popular vacation areas. To see migrating gray whales, try the west coast from California to British Columbia through the winter and spring. For sightings of endangered northern rights, there are tours from New Brunswick and Maine in late summer. To meet blue whales, the

best spot is the northern Gulf of St. Lawrence, Québec, in late summer or early autumn. And for leaping humpbacks – probably the most exciting species to watch – try the Cape Cod-Boston, Massachusetts, area from April to October or Hawaii throughout the winter. Contact provincial or state tourism offices for lists of whale-watching tour companies. A growing multi-million-dollar industry, whale watching has already proved that these giant sea creatures are far more valuable to humans alive than dead.

Here is a list of things to take along:
• A good camera – if possible, one with a telephoto lens – and a supply of Kodachrome 64 film if you want slides or Kodacolor 100, 200 or 400 if you want prints. The higher film speeds are particularly useful with a telephoto lens or on a cloudy day. Use black-and-white film if you plan to take photographs for research.
• Binoculars, if you have them.
• Sunscreen, even on a cloudy day. This will also help protect you from the wind. Take sunglasses and lip salve, as well.
• It may be necessary to use seasickness pills or "seasick patches."
• Warm clothes. Whales have thick blubber to keep them warm, but on the open sea, even when it is hot on land, you will need a coat, sweater or windbreaker – and maybe rain gear. It's best to go prepared.
• A waterproof packsack or other case to protect your camera, film, binoculars, clothes, snack and thermos containing a hot drink.
• This book, to help identify the whales you see.

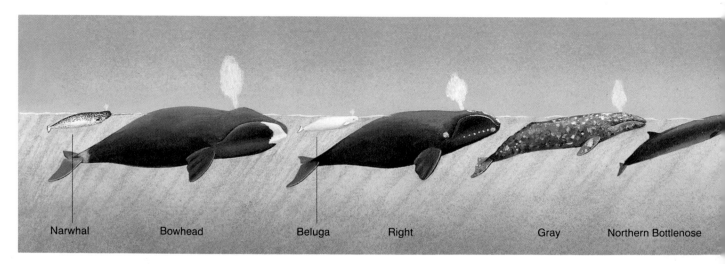

Narwhal   Bowhead   Beluga   Right   Gray   Northern Bottlenose

Identifying Whales at Sea

Whale watching, like bird watching, depends on the accurate identification of species. A whale is much larger than a bird but is often more difficult to identify because most of its body usually remains underwater. Most whale-watching trips have scientists or naturalists on board who will be happy to identify the whales you are likely to encounter.

The whale's spout is usually the first thing you see. Some individuals can be distinguished by the shape, size or angle of the spout. When you are closer, you may glimpse the animal's back, followed by its dorsal fin, if it has one, just after it spouts. Check the body shape above the surface. It is often the best clue you will get. If the whale jumps clear of the water, you will see its whole body, but you cannot count on every individual to jump. Finally, some whales lift their tail before diving. The tail, or fluke, shapes vary. Sometimes, this alone is enough to identify a humpback, northern right, sperm or blue whale,

but for other species, it may serve only as a clue. Other special features worth noticing are the narwhal's tusk, the white chin patch on the all-black bowhead, the white on the lower right side of the fin whale's head and the all-white body of the beluga.

You might want to keep a checklist of all the species you have seen, just as bird watchers do.

A whale watcher in the North Pacific, far left, reaches out to touch a friendly gray whale. At left, a humpback whale lifts its broad tail preparing to make a deep dive.

Compare the illustrations that run along the bottom of pages 62, 63, 64 and 65 to determine the species of whales you might meet at sea. The illustrations show the blow and overall body shape of each whale, as well as comparative sizes. Note that the flippers, flukes and dorsal fins vary in shape from species to species.

Some whales are found in every ocean, and others prefer only certain seas, depending on the ocean's temperature and depth, the food available and the season.

In the North Pacific, you can find blue, fin, sei, Bryde's, minke, humpback, gray and northern right whales; sperm, pygmy sperm and dwarf sperm whales; Baird's beaked, Cuvier's beaked and other beaked (*Mesoplodon*) whales.

In the North Atlantic, there are blue, fin, sei, Bryde's, minke, humpback and northern right whales; sperm, pygmy sperm and dwarf sperm whales; beluga whales (St. Lawrence River only); northern bottlenose whales, Cuvier's beaked and other beaked (*Mesoplodon*) whales.

In the Arctic, you might see belugas and narwhals; bowhead, minke and gray whales; and northern bottlenose whales.

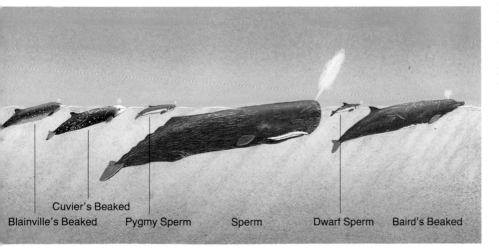

Cuvier's Beaked
Blainville's Beaked   Pygmy Sperm   Sperm   Dwarf Sperm   Baird's Beaked

How to Photograph a Whale at Sea

- Try to photograph close up any special markings, such as nicked dorsal fins, ragged tail flukes and scars or colour patches on the back.
- Take several photographs of each side of the whale, ideally with the sun at your back for best lighting.
- It is essential to take sharp photographs. If you are on a ship, use a fast shutter speed – at least 1/125 second and 1/1000 if possible. Hold the camera steady, or brace it when shooting.
- Note the time, day and place and the shot number on your camera.
- Once your films are printed, if you think you may have a valuable photograph – a shot of a rare species or of a well-marked whale – contact an office of the Department of Fisheries and Oceans (DFO) in Canada or the National Marine Fisheries Service (NMFS) in the United States. Or contact one or more of the research groups listed below that work on the species you have photographed.

Blue whales and minke whales (Atlantic):

- Mingan Island Cetacean Study, 285 Green Street, St-Lambert, Québec, Canada J4P 1T3

Humpback whales and fin whales (Atlantic):
- Center for Coastal Studies, Box 826, Provincetown, Massachusetts, U.S.A. 02657
- Department of Biology, Dalhousie University, Coburg Road, Halifax, Nova Scotia, Canada B3H 4H6
- Allied Whale, College of the Atlantic, Bar Harbor, Maine, U.S.A. 04609

Belugas (St. Lawrence):
- St. Lawrence National Institute of Ecotoxicology, 310, avenue des Ursulines, Rimouski, Québec G5L 3A1

Sperm whales:
- Department of Biology, Dalhousie University, Coburg Road, Halifax, Nova Scotia, Canada B3H 4H6
- Wildlife and Conservation Research Unit, Department of Zoology, Oxford University, South Parks Road, Oxford OX1 3PS, U.K.

Northern right whales:
- New England Aquarium Right Whale Project, New England Aquarium, Central Wharf, Boston, Massachusetts, U.S.A. 02110
- Department of Zoology, University of Guelph, Guelph, Ontario, Canada N1G 2W1

Gray whales and humpback whales (Pacific):
- West Coast Whale Research Foundation, Box 384, Tofino, British Columbia, Canada V0R 2Z0

Beaked whales:
- National Museum of Natural History, Smithsonian Institution, 10th Street and Constitution Avenue NW, Washington, D.C., U.S.A. 20560

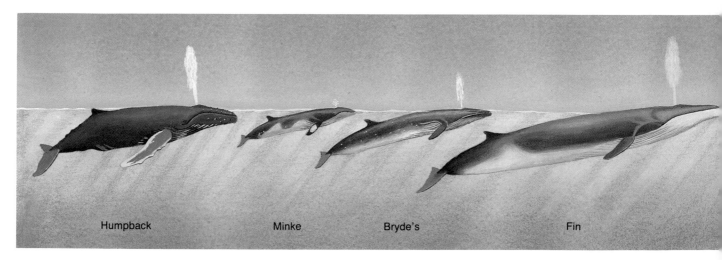

Humpback   Minke   Bryde's   Fin

A humpback whale, far left, waves its giant flipper—at up to five metres, it is the longest "arm" in the animal kingdom. Here in the Gulf of St. Lawrence, Richard Sears and his team of researchers from the Mingan Island Cetacean Study take whale watchers to meet humpbacks, fins, minkes and the largest whale of all, the blue. Whale watchers, whose fees help pay the cost of research, can share the delights and difficulties of studying animals that are constantly on the move, travelling through often rough and wind-curled seas. Yet to see the whales close up from a small boat is worth the discomfort. Whale watchers are treated to some exciting science in action. Some whale watchers have even taken photographs that have proved valuable for identification of individual animals.

At left, belugas seem to gather for a family portrait in the Canadian Arctic off Baffin Island. The darker-coloured calves are jumping beside and on the backs of their mothers.

In many places where whales swim close to land, it is possible to take good photographs from shore. The great advantage over shooting from boats is that tripods and a longer telephoto lens can be used. But even without a tripod, any action can be better photographed—as well as quietly observed—from shore.

Sei

Blue

How smart are whales? How does their intelligence compare with that of humans? While many scientists place the intelligence of the toothed species somewhere between that of a dog and a chimpanzee, other researchers admit that they simply do not have an answer.

Without any doubt, whales have large brains. The sperm whale has the largest brain of all—slightly larger than an elephant's and about five times the size of a human's. Both whales and humans have a complex cerebral cortex and are able to process a wide variety of information and to learn. But how can we measure cetacean intelligence? Will humans ever be able to communicate with whales?

Such questions are difficult to answer. First, we must consider the separate evolutionary paths of whales and humans. Humans evolved on land and spent millions of years in trees, where they developed the use of hands—including the opposable thumb. That adaptation, in turn, led to the invention of tools with which to perform tasks and build things. Human voices, developing in response to a need to communicate in a forest environment, were adapted for making a wide variety of sounds, including words, which led to the creation of language. Whales, having chosen the water, used paddle-shaped fins instead of hands. Their need as social mammals to communicate in a dark, watery environment led to the evolution of many specialized structures for making and hearing sounds.

As we have seen, the ability to hear, to make sounds and to echolocate varies widely from one cetacean species to the next. In general, the toothed whales, such as the sperm, beluga and narwhal, and the dolphins seem to make the most sophisticated use of sound. At least some learn the sounds of their species through mimicry. The killer whale even has dialects—sounds unique to a family group, which differ from those of neighbouring whales. Among all other animals, only humans share that ability.

In recent studies in Hawaii, captive dolphins were trained to respond to and communicate with humans, thereby proving that they have a good memory for sound and are able to imitate sounds and learn through observation. They were also able to form, generalize and learn rules, as well as to symbolize, form and act upon abstract concepts. One researcher taught a captive dolphin, already trained to accept fish as a reward, to do a new trick anytime it wanted a fish. The dolphin suddenly became very creative. In other experiments, dolphins were able to learn gestures as well as human words and to respond to them. These remarkable abilities, however, do not prove that dolphins have a language or have any need for one.

Since it is impossible to keep large whales in captivity, experimental work with the larger species must proceed much more slowly. Yet there are fascinating glimpses in current research that hint at the possibility of future contact between species. One such incident occurred recently in a study of sperm whales in the wild.

The researchers, led by Jonathan Gordon, had been following the whales near the Azores Islands in the North Atlantic. When the subjects stopped, a young American scientist, Lisa Steiner, jumped into the water and swam toward them. The whales —perhaps two dozen females and young— lay at the surface, their foreheads facing toward the centre. Japanese whalers had called this the "daisy" or "marguerite" formation and considered it a defensive posture. But Gordon and Steiner found that the whales came together every day in this position to socialize. At these times, they were often vocal.

As Steiner swam toward the group, one member turned to her, as if inviting her to join them. In a tender gesture that seemed to cross the language barrier between species, Steiner touched the animal. While friendly whales may only be curious about new things in their environment—in this case, a human—that curiosity may also be a deeper urge to socialize with humans. The researchers were left to ponder exactly what was going on inside those great heads.

American scientist Amy Knowlton, far left, reaches out to touch the callosities of a friendly right whale in the Bay of Fundy, a summer feeding and nursery area for mothers and youngsters in the North Atlantic. Northern right whales are the most endangered whales on Earth. Only 300 to 350 are left in the North Atlantic and perhaps only 200 in the North Pacific. Fortunately, researchers have photographically identified most of those remaining. It is only through knowing them and following their activities that researchers can hope to ensure their survival. The bond between humans and right whales may be crucial to their future.

At left, American scientist Lisa Steiner swims with sperm whales near the Azores Islands. Researchers here are only beginning to know these whales as individuals. Unlike northern right whales, sperm whales are not endangered, so the researchers have more time.

Sperm whale research has a fascinating quest: to uncover the complex social life of the largest brained animals on Earth. After hunting and killing them for so many years, humans might yet learn a great deal from sperm whales. Who knows what they might have to teach us?

Whales & the Future of the World Ocean

When a whale washes up dead on the beach, the questions begin. Why did it die? Was it because of disease, old age, pollution, a boat collision, or did the whale become entangled in fishing gear? Was it a combination of these factors? Scars or fishnet marks on the skin may tell us something, but often, there is no outward sign. Scientists faced with a 35-tonne carcass must overcome the daunting logistics of doing an autopsy on a whale. Unfortunately, they are usually able to find very little that is conclusive.

It is important, however, to investigate whale deaths and to find out as much as we possibly can about their causes. Because whales are at, or near, the top of the food chain, contaminants tend to concentrate in their body tissues. The fish-eating whales and other marine mammals that feed close to shore – a highly visible group which includes toothed whales and dolphins, seals and sea lions – are the first to show the effects of ocean pollution. If they are breeding and apparently happy, we know the ocean is healthy. If they are dying, washing up dead or no longer present in an area, the sea may be in trouble.

In recent years, the ocean has been used increasingly as a dump for human and industrial waste. Most marine pollution comes from the land – farms, city sewage systems, factories, nuclear reactors and oil refineries. Pesticides and other chemicals enter the rivers, first killing life there before flowing out to sea. Because of its sheer size, the sea can handle some of this waste. Ocean currents help dilute the effect of pollution, and some of it breaks down over time, but that can take many years. Studies show that at the current level of dumping, the ocean may not be able to break down or absorb such materials as toxic chemicals and radioactive waste.

In late 1987 and early 1988, at least 14 humpbacks and 750 bottlenose dolphins washed up dead along the east coast of the United States. After two years of study and millions of dollars for laboratory analysis, scientists found that the humpbacks had probably died of food poisoning. In separate and unrelated events, the dolphins and humpbacks had eaten fish carrying biotoxins.

Biotoxins are naturally occurring toxins from the occasional overproduction of certain species of red plankton, which creates what is commonly called a "red tide." The plankton, or red-tide organisms, which are so concentrated that they turn the water red, produce the toxin. When some fish eat enough of the plankton,

they die. Other fish, shellfish and plankton survive, but when they are eaten, the toxin travels up the food chain to large marine mammals.

Buried in the report on the dolphins, however, were results of laboratory tests showing that many of the dolphins carried very high levels of such chemical compounds as organochlorines, including PCBs, in their blubber and body organs. It is difficult to tell how high these levels must be to prove dangerous or toxic for a whale. Yet PCBs, by-products of manufacturing that break down very slowly in the environment, are known to suppress the immune systems of animals and humans, making them susceptible to disease.

Perhaps the PCBs weakened the dolphins, and the red-tide biotoxins then killed them. Other scientists think that pollution may be solely responsible for these deaths and the deaths of many other adult dolphins and whales, as well as the newborn calves of various whale species. Some believe it may be because the babies receive concentrated doses of contaminants through their mothers' milk.

There is only one ocean, and all the world's water cycles through it. Unless more research is done and more laws against ocean dumping are passed, the sea will become a deadly cocktail of chemicals and other contaminants. Although the ocean is vast, it is not bottomless; if we pollute one part of it, in time, the pollution will inevitably spread.

To save the whales, it is not enough simply to stop killing them. We must protect their habitat. On this planet, which is three-quarters ocean, we are finding that our own survival relies on clean water for fish and other future food supplies. Our survival as a humane species also depends on our care of the Earth and all its inhabitants. If we cannot save the whales and their ocean home, how can we hope to save ourselves?

The illustration, far left, shows how contaminants move up the food chain. The contaminants enter at the bottom levels and are often taken up along with nutrients by phytoplankton—microscopic plants that are the basis of all life in the sea. The phytoplankton are then eaten by animal plankton, or zooplankton, which are in turn eaten by fish, shellfish and baleen whales. If the contaminants are not too concentrated, they may not harm or kill animals till they reach the highest levels of the food chain, usually fish-eating toothed whales, dolphins, porpoises, seals and sea lions.

When whales eat contaminated food, the contaminants enter the digestive system. Because most contaminants cannot be broken down or eliminated through the normal metabolic pathways, they accumulate in tissues, mainly in the blubber. If and when the animal uses up its fat store, these contaminants become activated and can then cause damage, moving around the body from tissue to tissue. The PCBs and DDT are fat-based. Mercury, cadmium, arsenic and copper enter organs rather than blubber. Lead and zinc can accumulate in either fats or organs.

Alaskan Eskimos rally around gray whales caught in the ice near Point Barrow, Alaska, left. For two weeks in the autumn of 1988, the United States Air Force and Coast Guard, Greenpeace, the Alaskan National Guard and the government of the Soviet Union joined the Eskimos in working to free a couple of gray whales at an estimated cost of $1.3 million (U.S.).

Credits

p. 4 Doc White/Ocean Images Inc.
p. 5 John K.B. Ford
p. 6 James D. Watt/Earthviews
p. 7 (top) Al Giddings/Ocean Images Inc.
p. 7 (bottom) Fred Bruemmer
p. 8 François Gohier
p. 9 Scott Kraus/New England Aquarium
p.10 The Bettman Archive
p.11 Fred Bruemmer
p.14 (top) Richard Sears/MICS-Photo
p.14 (bottom) Jeff Foott/Bruce Coleman Inc.
p.17 Eda Rogers/Marine Mammal Images
p.18 Pieter Folkens
p.19 François Gohier
p.20 François Gohier
p.21 (top) François Gohier
p.21 (bottom) Kenneth C. Balcomb/Earthviews
p.22 Cartography by Margo Stahl
p.23 François Gohier
p.25 Jeff Foott
p.27 Howard Suzuki/Earthviews
p.30 François Gohier
p.31 François Gohier
p.33 Richard Sears/MICS-Photo
p.35 Kenneth C. Balcomb
p.37 Amy Knowlton/New England Aquarium
p.39 John K.B. Ford
p.41 Flip Nicklin
p.43 Robert Pitman/Earthviews
p.44 John Woestendiel/Earthviews
p.48 John K.B. Ford
p.49 Fred Bruemmer
p.51 Jeff Foott
p.52 (left) Flip Nicklin
p.52 (right) Jeff Foott/Valan Photos
p.53 (top) François Gohier
p.53 (bottom) Flip Nicklin
p.54 R.S. Wells
p.55 John K.B. Ford
p.56 (top) Flip Nicklin
p.56 (bottom) Flip Nicklin
p.57 Flip Nicklin
p.58 Des & Jen Bartlett/Bruce Coleman Inc.
p.59 Kelly Balcomb Bartok/Earthviews
p.60 Jonathan Gordon
p.61 Al Giddings/Ocean Images Inc.
p.62 Pieter Folkens
p.63 John Hyde/Bruce Coleman Inc.
p.64 J.M. Williamson
p.65 John K.B. Ford
p.66 Gregory Stone/New England Aquarium
p.67 International Fund for Animal Welfare
p.69 François Gohier

Further Reading

The Book of Whales
R. Ellis
Knopf, New York, 1980

A Field Guide to the Whales, Porpoises and Seals of the Gulf of Maine and Eastern Canada: Cape Cod to Newfoundland
S.K. Katona, V. Rough and D.T. Richardson
Scribner's, New York, 1983

A History of World Whaling
D. Francis
Viking, Markham, Ontario, 1990

The Natural History of Whales & Dolphins
P.G.H. Evans
Facts on File, New York, 1987

Orca: The Whale Called Killer
E. Hoyt
Camden House Publishing, 1990

The Sierra Club Handbook of Whales and Dolphins
S. Leatherwood, R.R. Reeves and L. Foster
Sierra Club Books, San Francisco, 1983

Voyage to the Whales
H. Whitehead
Chelsea Green, Vermont, 1989

The Whale Watcher's Handbook
E. Hoyt
Doubleday, New York, and Penguin/Madison Press, Toronto, 1984

Whales, Dolphins and Porpoises
Edited by R. Harrison and M.M. Bryden
Merehurst, London, 1988

The World's Whales: The Complete Illustrated Guide
S.M. Minasian, K.C. Balcomb III and L. Foster
Smithsonian Books, Washington, D.C., 1984

Also recommended is a magazine entirely devoted to whales: **Whalewatcher** from The American Cetacean Society, Box 4416, San Pedro, California, U.S.A. 90731

Conversion Chart

To Change	Into	Multiply by
centimetres	inches	0.4 (0.394)
metres	feet	3 (3.28)
kilometres	miles	0.6 (0.62)
sq. kilometres	sq. miles	0.4 (0.386)
kilograms	pounds	2.2 (2.205)
Celsius	Fahrenheit	1.8 and add 32

Index